Wine, Bach, and Cuckoo Clocks

Wine, Bach, and Cuckoo Clocks

Lorna Stuber

No part of this publication may be reproduced, distributed, or transmitted in any form or by any means—including photocopying, recording, or other electronic or mechanical methods—or by any information storage and retrieval system without the prior written permission of the author, except in the case of very brief quotations embodied in critical reviews and certain other non-commercial uses permitted by copyright law.

Cover Design: MiblArt

Interior Layout and Formatting: Lorna Stuber

Audiobook Narration: Rebecca H. Lee

ISBN paperback: 978-1-7778954-6-4

ISBN ebook: 978-1-7778954-7-1

ISBN audiobook: 978-1-7778954-8-8

Copyright ©2025 by Lorna Stuber. All rights reserved.

Disclaimer

I have done no formal research into my family history beyond reviewing the documents in my possession that have been compiled by extended family members. The history in this book also reflects conversations with relatives who remember more about our ancestors than I do.

I have also relied on my own memories and general knowledge of the migration of Germans from Germany to Russia and then to the US and Canada. The information about this history may not be 100 percent accurate. It is accurate to the best of my memories and informal research.

Dedication

To Great-Grandpa Emil Krause,

For your bravery in venturing across the Atlantic as a young man in the early 1900s. Because of the choice you made long ago, I was born in Canada and was given the opportunity to build the life I enjoy. I'm so grateful I was able to know you.

Contents

Royal Roots	1
Breaking Down the Wall	7
Getting Cultured	11
Guys Whose Names Start with R	17
East Meets West	23
Death Lives Here	29
The Best and Wurst of Nuremberg	35
The Stüber Hotel	41
A Little Cuckoo	53
Mother Knows Best	63
The Tears of Millions	71
Cruising the Baltic Sea	79
The Baltic Plague	87
Wine Time	97
Christmas in the Nick of Time	109
In Search of David	119
Martin Luther's Fifteen Minutes	139
Cousins by the Dozen	147
Food: The Universal Language	153
Afterword	159
Acknowledgements	161
About the Author	163
Also by Lorna Stuber	165
Voyages under the Midnight Sun	167
Endnotes	171

Royal Roots

I remember my mom telling me when I was a child that I descended from royalty. One document in the stack of Mom's belongings is a long and complicated family tree that does indicate a König (king), Prinz (prince), and several Prinzessin (princesses) in our family as far back as the 400s. I don't fully understand the document because of its complexity and the number of lines and names and titles—but it's good enough for me to prove that I am a German princess.

Until I was well into my forties, the oldest person I knew was my great-grandpa Emil Krause, who died when he was ninety-four years old and I was fourteen. He was my grandma's father on my mother's side and the only great-grandparent I remember. His first wife died when I was a baby, and my other great-grandparents died before I was born. My ancestors on both my mother's and father's side were all German, and my great-grandparents all migrated to Canada in the early 1900s seeking freedom and greater prosperity.

Great-Grandpa Krause was born in Tarutina, a small town in what is now Ukraine. When he lived there, the area was part of Bessarabia and under Russian control. Tarutina, a small colony of German settlers, was established in 1814. The soil in this area and around the Volga, where other German migrants settled, was good for farming, and the new residents grew wheat, corn, barley, and oats. They raised cattle, horses, and sheep. When Great-Grandpa was born in 1890, his extended family had a prominent presence in Tarutina with two men having served as mayor before he was born: Ferdinand from 1871-1874 and 1878-1881, August from 1887-1890. Ferdinand's son, Ferdinand II, was mayor from 1908-1911.

According to my mom, Great-Grandpa came to Canada at nineteen because he was going to be drafted into the Russian army.

"I'm not Russian. I don't speak Russian. I'm not going to fight for those damn Russians." (I have since learned that he did speak some Russian, but the sentiment is clear: He identified as a German man.)

And so he left Russia on March 29, 1909, and arrived at Ellis Island on May 6 of the same year. From there, he travelled to North Dakota, where he worked for a year, and then he took a train to Alberta. A document titled "Declaration of Intention," issued by the Department of Commerce and Labor in the Bureau of Immigration of Naturalization in the US, indicates that it was his "bona fide intention to renounce forever all allegiance and fidelity to any foreign prince, potentate, state, or sovereignty, and particularly to Nicholas II, Emperor of all the Russias."

My great-grandpa had strong foresight; five years after he left Russia, war broke out between Russia and Germany. In Russia, the Germans, even though they had been there for generations, were seen as enemies, traitors, and even spies. Nicholas II ordered Bessarabian and Volgan Germans to be exiled to Siberia, and he appropriated their lands. German people were prohibited from using the German language in all but the Volga region. No wonder my great-grandpa renounced the Czar.

Records belonging to my mom, such as copies of birth and marriage certificates, family trees, and family histories written by extended family members, indicate that my ancestors were Lutheran in the 1800s and early 1900s. How far back that religious affiliation goes I don't know, but the Thirty Years' War from 1618-1648, which renewed conflict between the Catholics and Protestants in Germany, may have prompted some of my ancestors to migrate to what was Prussian Poland in the late 1700s. (Poland had disappeared at this time, having been absorbed by Austria, Russia, and Prussia.) Some of these ancestors came from lower Saxony, where Martin Luther lived and worked.

Those ancestors were part of the mass migration prompted by Catherine II's 1763 manifesto inviting Germans to relocate to Russia. The manifesto granted them special rights and privileges as incentives to entice them to move: freedom of religion, exemption from paying taxes, free land, and other supports to help them establish homes and the means to make a living in their new homeland.[1] The timing of her manifesto coincided with tough times in Germany: drought, religious conflict, and high inflation, so thousands of Germans made the journey across the Baltic Sea or by train through Poland.

In 1871, less than twenty years before my great-grandpa was born, Czar Alexander II withdrew the privileges the German colonists had enjoyed up to then, including the men being exempt from military service. All men twenty-one and older were suddenly required to serve for four to seven years.[2] Many of the German men, including my great-grandpa, had limited or no Russian language skills and saw themselves as Germans rather than Russians. Added to the struggle was the famine of 1891-1892, which followed six years of bad harvests in the Volga. As a result, thousands of young men crossed the Atlantic to North and South America where, as had been the case earlier in Russia, greater opportunities were offered to them. In 1862, the US passed a law granting free land for agricultural use in the west, so once again, these farmers were on the move in search of a home with better opportunities. Between 1880-1920, more than twenty-five million German migrants left Russia.[3] Roughly one million of them settled in the US, Canada, and South America. All of my great-grandparents were among them.

My mother's grandparents on her father's side, also Lutheran, were already married and had two young children when they immigrated to Canada and established a farmstead on the Alberta prairies, beginning their new life on a new continent.

My father's ancestral history is similar to that of my mother's family: Mom and Dad were both descendants of Germans who migrated to Bessarabia and ultimately relocated to Canada, where they became farmers on the prairies. Maybe, somewhere back in the lineage, I'm related to myself.

A copy of Great-Grandpa Krause's certificate of naturalization shows he became "naturalized as a British subject" in "the Province of Alberta in the Dominion of Canada" in 1914. His wife, my great-grandma, was born in Lichtental, Bessarabia. They married in Alberta in 1912. My great-grandpa never saw his parents or many of his siblings again after leaving Europe when he was nineteen.

From as early as I can remember, probably age three or four, I was fascinated by this soft-spoken, mostly bald, blue-eyed, shriveled-up old man with thick black-framed glasses and who spoke a different language whenever we saw him. I don't remember him ever wearing anything other than a black suit with a white shirt. When I was old enough to understand that he had been born in a mysterious, faraway land, I became curious about what that land was like. I wanted to hear his stories, to hear him describe the landscape and his life in his homeland, and to connect to my family's history. Despite living in Canada for more than seventy years, he seemed more comfortable speaking German than English, and he only spoke German when my mom, my grandma, and I were visiting him. I only knew a smattering of German words, so I could never ask him my flurry of questions.

After meeting him a few times, I wanted to learn more than just the few German words my parents and grandparents had taught me so that I could talk to him, but I only had the chance to study German as a high school student, two years after he died.

During those early years, I didn't recognize the finer details of my life that were connected to this mysterious old man—and the great-grandparents I had never met, and the culture they had brought with them. For me, it was normal for Santa to come to our house during the early evening on Christmas Eve rather than overnight while we were asleep. I never experienced waking up on Christmas morning excited to see presents under the tree. Instead, my parents planted our presents while my sister and I were changing in or out of our Christmas dresses on the evening of the 24th before we went to church or after we had come home. Once my sister and I were in our pajamas, we were allowed to sprint to the tree to see what Santa had brought while we were at church. According to my mom, Santa had also stuffed our stockings while we were at church. It wasn't until I was older that I realized that my friends who were not of German descent didn't celebrate Christmas on the 24th.

Christmas wasn't the only time German and Eastern European traditions were part of our lives. Some of my favourite foods growing up, and to this day, are cabbage rolls, stewed pork with cabbage, sauerkraut, homemade garlic sausage, and potato-everything throughout the year, especially potato salad. But Christmas was the only time of year we got the special stuff: pickled herring and all of my grandmas' German cookies: Pfeffernusse, Lebkucken, Kulleraugen (thumbprint cookies).

I would have loved to have asked my great-grandpa what Christmas was like for him as a child. Even though Bessarabia was where he was born and raised, I've always felt connected to Germany. He was a temporary transient in Bessarabia, but his ties to Germany remained strong. He brought to Canada the language, food, Christmas traditions, religion, and the work ethic that I saw in all members of my family while I was growing up. The desire to learn my family's history gripped me, and somewhere during my childhood, my mom and I made a pact to go to Germany together one day.

We were able to check that goal off the list when I was in my late thirties while visiting a friend in Saxony, part the former East Germany where some of my ancestors had migrated from to Russia, touring historical sites in Nuremburg and Munich, and exploring the area near Stuttgart, where some of my mom's other ancestors originated. Our trip to Germany was my first of multiple visits to the land of my origins, and I continue to visit when I can to spend time with a long-time friend and to enjoy what has become a second home. I go to reconnect with a part of myself that I have always felt closer to when I'm in the country of my ancestors.

I may never get a chance to live in Germany; living there and studying German for six months to a year has been one of my goals since my teenage years, but as I grow older, I wonder if I will ever get to check that off my list. Regardless, each time I visit Germany, I learn more about the culture, history, and my ancestral connections to the country. And damn, a pork Schnitzel pounded good and thin and glass of crisp Rhein Reisling schmeckt gut (taste good)!

Breaking Down the Wall

In 2000, I was teaching English to international students at a private language school in downtown Calgary. Most of our students were young adults—university students or young professionals—coming to Canada for an average of one to three months for intensive English study and homestay.

I worked at that school for five and a half years, teaching all levels of English and specialized programs: business English and TOEIC and TOEFL test preparation classes. When the school also began offering Cambridge English Exam prep courses, I jumped at the chance to teach those too. (TOEFL, TOEIC, and Cambridge Exams are standardized tests of English language proficiency for those who have learned English as a second, third, etc. language. They measure reading, writing, listening, and speaking skills, and a minimum score is required to be considered fluent enough to enroll in an English-speaking university or to be hired for some jobs.)

The Cambridge course I was teaching in the fall of 2000 had only six students in it. One of them was a young dentist from Germany who wanted to obtain her Cambridge certificate and then practice dentistry in an English-speaking country. Christine was only a few years younger than I was, and when she learned that my ancestry was German, we started chatting outside of class. She grew up in the former East Germany and was fifteen when the Berlin Wall came down and the two parts of Germany reunified.

I had had a pen pal in my early teenage years from the former West Germany, and growing up in the 1970s during the Cold War, I had always been curious about the hidden societies of East Germany, the USSR, and other Eastern Block countries. In Canada, we had been taught that these countries and the people in them were "the enemy" and were not to be trusted, yet in front of me was a funny, pleasant, friendly woman close to my age who felt more like a relative than a possible foe.

Wine, Bach, and Cuckoo Clocks

Christine first visited Canada as a teenager shortly after the Wall came down. She had pre-booked transportation from the Vancouver airport to her hotel, but in her naïveté, she had unknowingly booked a limo not a taxi. Minutes into the drive, she knocked on the window and asked the driver if she could join him up front because she was lonely.

During her first trip to Canada, Christine spawned a friendship with an older woman from Vancouver who was sitting beside her on the plane from Germany. The woman somewhat adopted her, inviting Christine to stay with her on subsequent trips to Canada. By 2000, the woman was living in south Calgary. The offer of accommodation with a friend coupled with the fact that she found a school that was offering Cambridge courses brought Christine to Calgary and to my class.

Our friendship was solidified when Christine realized what a goofball I am. Near the end of the course, I took a Friday off to head to Las Vegas for the first time with a co-worker during the National Finals Rodeo. It was a last-minute, spontaneous trip, so we hadn't secured rodeo tickets. We never made it *to* the rodeo, but we wanted to go *during* the rodeo to take in the atmosphere.

My friend insisted that we walk up and down the Strip to see all of the themed hotels, inside and out. We also went to the Cowboy Christmas exhibit and show at the Las Vegas Convention Center, walking to the Convention Center and back to our hotel instead of taking a taxi. All of this in our cowboy boots. By the time we ended our three-day trip, my feet were so sore from all the walking on asphalt in cowboy boots that I put maxi pads in the bottoms of my boots to give my feet a bit of cushion.

When I reported for work on Monday, I spent the day in slippers instead of shoes. While relaying some of our travel stories to my class, Christine laughed heartily, realizing her teacher was someone who shared her dry, warped sense of humour and, like her, rolled with whatever life brought forth.

After Christine returned to Germany, we kept in touch. The following summer, when she returned to Alberta, we toured places in Calgary and surrounding area that she hadn't been to yet. Thus began our tradition of getting together somewhere in the world once a year with either her visiting Calgary or me visiting Germany. In the years since, we have expanded our meeting points, vacationing together in Mexico, the Caribbean, or elsewhere.

When she visits Canada, I aim to take her to places she hasn't been, travelling farther from Calgary and exploring other parts of Alberta and BC. She has a paper Alberta road map and has highlighted every highway and secondary road we have been on; her goal is to highlight every road on the map.

Part of our tradition involves "liver training," as she calls it—a gradual increase of alcohol intake on both of our parts leading up to our visits so that when we get together, we are ready to handle daily consumption of good wine and other tasty beverages. In Canada, I push glasses of Canadian wines her way (wines from Heaven's Gate, The Vibrant Vine, and other favourite Okanogan wineries), and when I'm in Germany, of course I sample the local beers and wines since Germany has countless high-quality versions of both.

A week prior to Christmas 2024, Christine sent me a meme through WhatsApp that said, "If a friendship lasts longer than fifteen years, you're no longer friends. You're family."

I responded with one word: "True."

Getting Cultured

I'm a hick.

In the early 1990s, I spent three years living in Fujisawa, a small city forty-five minutes by train from the heart of Tokyo. The population of Fujisawa at the time was around 300,000—the biggest city I had lived in up to that point.

In 2011, on my first trip to New York City, I decided I didn't want to go to Broadway shows every night, so for one evening, I splurged on a ticket for the opening night of the New York Philharmonic's season. Among the people I saw, I was the only person not wearing a tuxedo or full-length ball gown. I was dressed up but not enough to be described as "black tie."

When I went to Sydney, Australia in 2019, I bought ticket for a concert in the Opera House. I had been hiking in the Blue Mountains during the day and managed to make it back to the city and to the Opera House to take my seat two minutes before the concert began. I had a change of nice clothes in my day pack, but I didn't have time to change. I enjoyed the concert in my hiking boots and shorts.

I've eaten some atrociously expensive meals at swanky restaurants in Las Vegas, and I've been appropriately dressed for those meals. It's not out of the realm of possibility for me to get dolled up in expensive shoes and nice clothes and behave myself in a fancy restaurant or attend a symphony concert.

But I'm still a hick.

One of the running jokes Christine and I have is that somewhere on our agenda, we need to find "some culture," which for me often involves a rodeo, a hike in the Rocky Mountains, a country music concert, or a visit to one of Alberta's most treasured tourist attractions such as the world's largest sausage (a forty-two foot tall statue of a kolbasa in Mundare, Alberta) or the whimsical and budget-friendly World Famous Gopher Hole Museum in Torrington, Alberta.

The gopher museum is in a building roughly the size of a two-car garage and is the main tourist attraction in Torrington, Alberta (population 306 according to the 2021 census), a one-hour drive from Calgary. (The fire hydrants in town are also painted to look like cartoon gophers.) The museum holds forty-four dioramas, each with taxidermied gophers depicted in various scenes: a hair salon, a curling game, a wedding, and much more. I took Christine and her husband, Alan, there on one of their visits to Canada and have taken other friends there as well. I could not convince my mom to go.

"Your grandma is always bugging me to take her," Mom used to tell me. "She really wants to see it."

"Why not? It's a short drive and would be a fun afternoon outing for her. And the admission is only two dollars."

"I'm not paying two dollars to see stupid little gophers in dresses!"

"Aw, come on! It's totally worth the two bucks. And the town apparently has it written in their bylaws that the price is never to go any higher than two dollars. You should go. It's a great exhibit of Alberta culture."

"Forget it."

But Christine and Alan loved it.

On one of Christine's other visits, I took her to Elk Island National Park, a small wilderness park packed with wooded marshes. The park is a thirty-minute drive east of Edmonton, and visitors can frequently see moose, elk, and bison roaming freely. We got a close-up glimpse of a bison as we were standing on the human side of the eight-foot fence enclosing the pasture. As we were admiring the massive beast from afar, he looked at us and started leisurely lumbering toward us, prompting us to burst out screaming and running for our lives back to the car. He had probably only taken eight steps by the time we had bolted 100 metres back to the car; he was completely nonplussed by our shrieks, but we were certain that death was imminent since the fence could not possibly be strong enough to protect us from his savage attack. Since that day, we have impressed people with our harrowing tale of how we were almost mauled and trampled by a WILD, RAGING BISON STAMPEDING TOWARD US and thank God we were able to outrun him!

"Culture" in Germany is a little different than it is in small-town Alberta. My first clue was when Christine was visiting Alberta in 2004 and I excitedly pointed out to her that "next year will be Alberta's 100th anniversary!" She burst out laughing and told me, "One hundred years of history is nothing. If you want to see literary, political, and architectural history, you need to go to Europe, where many of the buildings are centuries old."

In 2006, after Christine had come back to Canada a few times, it was my turn to visit her. And time to get real about that agreement my mom and I had made when I was a kid about going to Germany together.

I booked flights and started making plans with Christine for my first visit to my ancestral homeland. I was adamant that my mom come with me since we had talked for three decades about making this trip together. She hesitated and stalled, coming up with lame excuses, until I finally told her to just do it. I was going whether she came with me or not, and I would prefer that it was not "not." She finally succumbed to my pestering and booked a seat on the flight I was on.

I also convinced my mom that we should buy first-class rail passes as the price difference between first and second class was minimal. We would, after all, be travelling the whole country by train after getting off the plane in Frankfurt. She hadn't travelled nearly as much at that point in life as she had wanted to, so I told her, "This is your chance to enjoy Germany. We've talked about this for years and years. Let's spend a little extra and enjoy the better seats." She agreed.

***

When we landed in Frankfurt, I kicked into both teacher and international traveller modes since my mom was neither. Her travels outside of Canada and the US were limited to a few excursions to Mexico and a trip to Japan to visit me when I was living there. Even when she and I travelled to San Francisco a few years before our Germany trip, she left the organizing to me since I had more travel experience than she did.

I maneuvered us through the Frankfurt airport to the train ticket office, where we secured seats for our train ride to Torgau, three hours from Frankfurt.

"Here, Mom, this is our platform. We can wait here."

I double checked our tickets and yes, we were on the right platform.

We were an hour early, and there was already a train on the platform, seemingly not in any hurry to depart.

"I bet this is our train," I told her. "Maybe we can get on it and wait in our seats."

While I was peering at the numbers on the side of the train and comparing them to our tickets, a German man stopped, prompted by what must have been an obvious look of confusion on my face.

"Do you need some help?" he asked in English.

"I think this is our train but I'm not sure."

I showed him our tickets.

"Yes, this is the right platform, but this train is bound for Switzerland."

Ah. I was a little taken off guard. My travel-by-train experience was limited to Japan, and in Japan, obviously it was not possible to hop on a train and end up in a different country! I shook my head, reminding myself that this was *not* Japan, and I probably had a lot to learn about getting around Germany. I cooled my enthusiasm and sat us down to wait for our train.

As we travelled from Frankfurt to Torgau, I watched the corn fields and villages whizzing by and imagined what life would have been like in this countryside when my ancestors were still peasant farmers. The train made a few stops, and as we neared the three-hour mark, I noticed a slight change in the scenery. I assumed we had crossed over into what was the former East Germany because the buildings, fences, and bridges looked older, less maintained, more dreary. My mind drifted to growing up in Canada in the 1970s, during the Cold War, when countries like the USSR and East Germany were mysterious, unknown places. I remember being taught that the countries "behind the Wall" were enemies and that communism was evil. By the time our train entered the former East Germany, I was old enough to realize that people are people regardless of where they come from and that communism wasn't from Satan; it was just a different political system, much different from what I had ever lived in. I knew my good friend had survived fifteen years growing up in a communist state, and she didn't seem the least bit evil.

Still, I took mental note of the sometimes stark, sometimes subtle differences between the former West Germany and the Eastern region. There were no border controls, as there had been only a few years earlier, and it struck me how much one country can change even over the course of my lifetime, which was slightly more than thirty years at that point.

When the train pulled into Torgau, I noticed that the station buildings were blackened and the station was small. The concrete was old and worn.

Is the black on the buildings from age or fire or ...? I wondered.

Christine was on the platform waiting for us. She greeted us each with a big welcoming hug.

"Welcome to Germany and to Torgau! This is our train station."

"It looks old," I responded.

"That's putting it mildly. It's embarrassing!" she said as she laughed.

She and I had had several conversations over the years about her experiences growing up in the former East Germany. There are a few sensitive topics that I never bring up, so at her comment about her train station, I simply laughed, shrugged, and said, "Well, it serves its purpose. It got us here. That's all that matters."

When we arrived at Christine's parents' home in Torgau, they greeted us as warmly as she had. Her mother reminded me of my Auntie Sandra, with a similar hair style and colour (blonde, wavy, short, and cute), similar stature (slim and not too tall), and similar facial features. She was well put together and friendly although perhaps a little self-conscious about speaking English with these two guests from Canada. Christine's father also had the same warm vibe. I immediately felt welcome.

Christine showed us to our rooms and then the five of us launched into coffee and cake, the best of German traditions, in my opinion. During our stay with Christine's family, regardless of whether we were out and about or if we were in their home, all activity stopped at 4 pm for coffee and cake.

The cakes were varied; if we were in a coffee shop, our choices were anything from plain chocolate cake to decadent cheesecakes, pastries, or fruit cakes in the same style as the Kuchen my grandmas and mother made. I broke out into a wide smile at my first glimpse of plum Kuchen, a family favourite, here in front of me in my friend's parents' home, thousands of miles away from where I had always eaten it. I was thrilled to be enjoying a cake in the same form and with the same taste as my mom and grandmas had made for me countless times.

Mom and I sat with Christine and her parents, enjoying this German daily tradition, getting to know one another. Christine's parents' English was much better than they thought it was and certainly much better than my limited and my mom's non-existent German. My mom had told me when I was a kid that both she and my dad only spoke German when they were five years old and began school, but they had since lost the language entirely except for a few words like Kuchen or Scheisse—two of the important words (cake and shit).

But food is a universal tool that brings humans together.

Guys Whose Names Start with R

Christine was on a mission to show me and my mom some culture, so we headed to Dresden, 115 kilometres away. Getting there was doable by train, but Christine drove us. Anyone who hasn't been to Germany but has heard that there are no speed limits on the Autobahns, well ....

Christine drives the way Germans drive. Fast. But also safely. Knowing that my mother would prefer the front seat, I settled into the back, where my smirk was out of sight when I saw my mother digging her fingernails into the dash as Christine was cruising down the Autobahn at 180 kilometres per hour.

My comment, "Don't worry, Mom; she's a good driver," made Christine giggle and say, "I'm not even driving fast! I should be driving over 200 kilometres per hour!"

I think my mom's fingers almost broke off at that point.

Dresden is spilling over with culture and art. Prior to World War II, it was nicknamed "Florence on the Elbe" because of its richness in art, but much of the city was destroyed in the bombings. When the war ended, Dresden found itself behind the Iron Curtain and a debate ensued as to whether to level the city or reconstruct the Saxon royal palace and other historical buildings. The central, historical part of the city has been rebuilt.

Christine started our tour by showing us the Fürstenzug, a 101-metre-long mural depicting all of the rulers of Saxony over the centuries. It was here that I commented to Christine, "Ah yes, your history is a bit longer than Alberta's," as the mural itself has existed for well over a hundred fifty years, having been painted in the 1870s to celebrate the 800th anniversary of the Wettin Dynasty. (I recognize that the Indigenous Peoples have a long history on the American continents, and sites such as Head-Smashed-In Buffalo Jump and Writing on Stone, two of my favourites, near where I live depict this history.)

Wine, Bach, and Cuckoo Clocks

Dresden has been the capital city of Saxony for over 800 years. Saxony's greatest ruler was Augustus the Strong, who ruled from the late 1600s until his death in 1733. He "liked to show that he lived up to his name by breaking horseshoes with his bare hands and engaging in fox tossing by holding the end of his sling with just one finger while two of the strongest men in his court held the other end."[4] As a patron of the arts, Augustus was responsible for turning Dresden into the arts centre it remains today, building palaces and establishing extensive art collections, including a large collection of fine china produced in the royal factory in Meissen, near Dresden.

Snapping pictures as we went, Mom and I followed Christine through the Neumarkt, the central square in Dresden, which was almost entirely obliterated in bombings by the Allies in World War II. Here, Christine pointed to Augustus, a life-sized statue covered in gold leaf of him on horseback and dressed in Roman armour.

Christine had one building in mind as our ultimate destination: Gemäldegalerie Alte Meister, or Old Masters Picture Gallery. Old masters. And pictures. And a gallery. An art gallery? Culture!

I'm not a huge fan of museums, nor am I an art afficionado, but I thought, *Hey, we're in Europe, and Christine wants to show us this museum. Let's go for it.*

It takes me maybe half an hour to get bored inside any museum. After an hour of looking at old artifacts and reading plaques, I'm done. If there is more to see at that point, I blast through the rest of the building(s), glancing at the artifacts as I make my way to the exit. Ironic because I'm such a history buff and I'm fascinated by archaeology, but for some reason, objects inside a museum don't keep my interest for long. I'd much rather be traipsing along cobblestone streets looking at ruins and architecture.

I know little about art, so admittedly I wasn't appreciating the displays as much as others may until I noticed some names that made me pause. The vast majority of the names on the paintings were ones I hadn't heard of, but as soon as I saw "Rembrandt" I stopped and took a second glance.

The Rembrandt? *That guy? Am I really looking at one of his pieces?*

Yep, this was the real stuff.

Then I saw another name I recognized. Rafael. Lesser known to me, but I knew he was also a big deal in the art world.

Huh.

I continued, now more attentive.

And there was another.

Renoir.

What's going on here?

I had always thought I would have had to go to Italy or France to see these guys' works hanging in an art gallery. I looked at Christine, and she laughed.

"Are you getting enough culture?" she asked me.

"These are the real things?" I asked. "I'm looking at an actual Rembrandt painting with my own eyes?"

"Girl, we need to get you out of Alberta more often!" she teased me, as we continued through the gallery.

***

Fun fact: Rafeal was left-handed. So were Michelangelo, Van Gogh, da Vinci, and numerous other great artists, inventors, and influential people (Napoleon, Joan of Arc, Paul McCartney, some retired barber named Stu who lives two hours north of me). Whether Rembrandt was left-handed or not is still disputed. So far, eight US presidents have been left-handed, although the number may be higher because until the last several decades, lefties were forced to learn how to write and do other tasks with their right hands.

As a leftie, I'm always fascinated when I hear of other southpaws' achievements. It's nice to know I'm in good company.

***

I definitely reached my saturation point of culture after the art museum and touring the palace and viewing the fine china—porcelain *from* China and Meissen that Augustus had acquired—and the rest of his collection of fine goods. But Christine wasn't done trying to give me some class. Over the next four days, she toured me and Mom around several spots in her hometown, including the Villeroy & Boch warehouse, where she bought me a fine china teapot and matching teacups. I must admit, tea *does* taste better when drinking it out of good china rather than out of a manky old coffee cup. In future visits to Germany, Christine made a point of taking me to the Villeroy & Boch warehouse and I have since added to my collection of non-garage sale kitchenware: a set of four crystal white-wine glasses and an equally fine set of champagne flutes. During my last visit in 2024, she warned me, "Villeroy and Boch was just the foundation. I'm working up to taking you to Meissen, where you can make your own china cups and personalize them."

Christine's list of "cultural activities" also included taking us to dinner in Auerbachs Keller in Leipzig. "Goethe! You need to get in touch with your writing heroes," was her reasoning.

Johann Wolfgang von Goethe came to Leipzig in 1765 to study law. His drama *Faust* is partly set in Auerbachs Keller. Auerbachs Keller has always been a popular wine tavern for students. It is the second oldest restaurant in Leipzig and was frequented by Goethe when he was studying at Leipzig University from 1765-1768. There, he saw two paintings, one of which showed Johann Georg Faust drinking with students. The other depicted Faust riding a wine barrel out the door of the tavern. Legend says that he enlisted the devil to assist him in riding the barrel. "The scene Auerbach's Cellar in Leipzig in [Goethe's] drama *Faust I* is his literary memorial to his student tavern and to the city."[5]

True confession time: I haven't read *Faust*. Yet.

Goethe, Kafka, Nietzsche, Bach, Wagner. Many of the greats in literature, music, and other arts were born in, studied, or worked in Leipzig. Richard Wagner was born in Leipzig in 1814, and Nietzsche studied at the Leipzig University.

***

I was raised Evangelical, not Lutheran. Having learned about the Reformation in school and Sunday school, and knowing that my ancestors were Lutheran, I've always been interested in the details of the Reformation. It was, after all, one of the most significant turning points in Christian history.

Christine's hometown, Torgau, is on the banks of the Elbe River and has great historical significance in regards to the Reformation. Martin Luther began preaching in Torgau, and in 1530, along with Philipp Melanchthon, Justus Jonas, and Johannes Bugenhagen, he developed the Torgau Articles, which condemned abuses and corrupt practices of the Church of Rome. Torgau became the political centre of the Reformation. As a result, it is known as the wet-nurse of the Reformation whereas Wittenberg is said to be the mother. Christine tells me that the true translation from German to English states that Torgau was the cradle of the Reformation.

Martin Luther's wife, Katharina, died in Torgau in 1552 and is buried in the town's St. Mary's Church. The Katharina-Luther-Stube in Torgau, the house where Luther's wife died, is a museum dedicated to her.

On day three of our visit, Mom and I were treated to a private guided tour of the significant sites of the Reformation in Torgau. Christine had arranged for one of her neighbours to spend a couple of hours showing us around and giving us a historic explanation of the sites and events of Luther's time in the town. Having learned mainly of the nailing of his Ninety-Five Theses on the door of the Castle Church in Wittenberg, I had no idea that this small town had played such a significant behind-the-scenes role in the movement that Luther was spearheading at the time. Our social studies courses in school hadn't drilled down to that depth of detail. I also wasn't aware that the presence of the plague in Wittenberg had promoted the move of Reformation events to Torgau, fifty kilometres away.

This tour was much more in line with my idea of "culture" than the art museum. I love stories about religious, cultural, and political upheaval and change. I'd much rather listen to stories and observe buildings and landmarks where significant events took place than look at objects under glass or on walls in a museum. In addition, because my ancestors were Lutheran and some were from Saxony, I felt an even closer personal connection to Germany when we entered the "Lutheran" part of our vacation.

Wine, Bach, and Cuckoo Clocks

The Lutheran church in my hometown and its members were a significant part of my childhood. I had many classmates and friends who attended the church. One of my best friends was the adopted daughter of the Lutheran minister in town. The best homemade sausages of my life were those made by my parents and grandparents and the men in the Lutheran church. My family never missed the church's pancake supper on Shrove Tuesday every year while I was growing up as we knew we'd be treated to not only great pancakes and fun socializing, what with knowing everyone, but the men from the church always donated their homemade German sausages for the pancake supper.

Our Reformation-themed evening in Torgau ended with a meal at Herr Käthe Restaurant, a cozy café mere steps from Katharina-Luther-Stube featuring German cuisine. We got the "full-meal-deal," so to speak, having finished a walking tour and educational information on Luther's activities and how his wife is still revered in the town. We topped the day off with a delicious German meal (more sausages!). We were too full for dessert, but I was intrigued to order one item from the menu simply because of its name: Ikea Dessert. When I saw this at the top of the dessert menu card on the table, I asked Christine, "What does this mean? You order this, they bring the ingredients to the table, and you make your own dessert?"

She had no idea what it would entail, and sadly, none of us ordered it. I may have to have another meal at the restaurant one day so I can build my own dessert.

East Meets West

When I first met Christine, she introduced herself to people in Calgary as being from "near Leipzig" since many Albertans likely wouldn't have heard of Torgau. Leipzig to Torgau is less than an hour by train. Still, until I planned my first trip to Germany, I didn't have a good sense of where in the country she was from other it being the former East Germany. I knew Munich was in the south of Germany and Berlin was much further north and had been cut in two by the Wall.

But having grown up during the Cold War, I knew almost nothing about the former East Germany. One detail I remember hearing when I was a kid was that women from West Germany shaved their legs and armpits and women from East Germany didn't. I have no idea where I heard that—maybe it was simply speculation by a group of Canadian teenagers in the early 1980s to try to envision "those communists." Either that or it was likely one of those many pieces of Cold War propaganda floating around Canada and the US that served to keep us in fear of what was on the other side of the Iron Curtain—and I had no idea if it was true. Regardless of its source, it was one of those ridiculous details thrown around that made us think that the East Germans were less civilized than we were. But for the longest time, I believed it. Until I became an adult, saw the Wall come down, and started to see news clips of "those people from the East," I'd thought East Germans were closer to Neanderthals, terrorists, or spies than those of us living on this side of the Iron Curtain. (Oh the irony, now that I've been to that fancy schmancy art museum in Dresden.)

Looking back on my junior and senior high school studies, it surprises me that I didn't learn about Leipzig as a city with the historical significance it has; it was home to Johann Sebastian Bach from 1723 to 1750 and site of The Battle of Nations in 1813, which marked the end of Napolean's rule in Europe. If I learned any of this information in school while growing up, it didn't stick with me. A massive monument a ten-minute drive from city centre commemorates this battle. Christine took Mom and me to see it for some more "culture."

The front of the monument depicts a battle scene, which is bookended with two staircases leading to the entrance. Above the main door is a statue of the archangel Michael, symbolizing God's protection for the German soldiers. Twelve statues of warriors at the top of the monument represent freedom and justice. There is also an observation deck at the top.

As Christine toured us through this and other significant sites in what was formerly known as East Germany, I reflected on growing up during the Cold War and what I learned in history classes. I remembered thinking as a child and teenager that Russia could "nuke us" at any moment with no warning and believing that Canada, the US, and Western Europe were infiltrated with communist spies from the USSR and other Eastern European countries. My knowledge of the Protestant Reformation was pretty standard. I remembered hearing that Martin Luther nailed his Ninety-Five Theses on the door of the Castle Church in Wittenberg, and I recalled hearing what his grievances of the Roman Catholic Church were. I also knew who Napoleon and Bach were and why they were such famous figures.

But I realized on that tour that I hadn't learned the finer details of these men's lives. Was it because I was in school during a time that East Germany was perceived as "the enemy" with their affiliation with the USSR and communism? Or was it simply because our class time in history class was limited so to cover both Canadian and world history, our lessons about world history went wide rather than deep? Perhaps it was a bit of both.

Once I visited the former East Germany, I realized that while there are some differences, people from "the other side" are not monstrous, evil, and backward, as I had been led to believe. But their history was sobering. (When I asked Christine for her feedback on this part of the book, she tilted her head and said, "I don't know if 'sobering' would be the right word choice. As part of our coping, we learned to develop a taste for vodka—the good Russian vodka—so we certainly weren't 'sober.'")

People didn't have a lot, but they had what they needed.

"Sure, we had to line up in front of stores to buy our groceries," Christine said, "and every day, the stores had different amounts of bread, vegetables, and fruit. The selection wasn't consistent, but we didn't starve. There was always something on the shelves. And we also had our own plots where we could grow vegetables."

I was also under the impression that people's lives were determined by the government—that they were told which jobs to have, where to live, etc.

"Yes, to a certain extent, but it wasn't so strict," Christine told me in one of our first conversations. "We weren't given a choice in what our profession would be. I was told I was to be an Olympic swimmer until I got kicked off the swimming team. Sports were highly regarded and came with good benefits like extra food."

"You got kicked off the team? For some sort of political reason?" I asked her.

She laughed.

"No, for overtraining. I was working myself so hard during the practices that I always threw up beside the pool. My trainer eventually told my mother that I was working myself too hard and that perhaps I should try a different sport. She kicked me off the team, but it was only because she was tired of cleaning up my vomit."

Christine's parents were dentists, and she chose to also become a dentist. The Wall came down when she was still young enough that she hadn't been forced to follow a career path yet.

"The building our dental practice is in used to be the Stasi headquarters in Torgau. When we were doing renovations, we had to do some rewiring. The officials told us we could cut any of the wires we needed to. We cut one wire and suddenly the entire town was without telephone service. The wire we had cut was the main telephone line for the town that the Stasi had used to listen to people's telephone conversations."

The Stasi (Ministry of State Security, aka, the secret police in the former East Germany) was modelled after the KGB in Russia and like the KGB, it was a secretive and dangerous force. They recruited informants and had hundreds of thousands of people spying on and collecting information on their neighbours, friends, and even family members. No one could be trusted.

Wine, Bach, and Cuckoo Clocks

The Stasi Museum in Runde Ecke in Leipzig is a small but thought-provoking historical display of how controlled life was behind the Iron Curtain. It is located in the former Stasi headquarters, a building with a rounded front on the corner of a busy intersection—an ideal location from which to watch people on the street.

"I can't be in here," Christine said to me five minutes after we had entered the museum. She walked out.

I looked around for ten more minutes and then joined her, where she was sitting on the steps in front of the building. I left Mom inside to take her time viewing as much as she wanted to see.

"It just brings back too many memories," Christine said as she lifted her head and looked at the camera fixed on a light stand above our heads. Seeing the camera gave me chills. Even though I was used to seeing cameras in public places, this one had more significance. It was no longer used to spy on people; this was the typical camera used in current times to provide police with footage in case of car accidents or crime, but its presence and location had a much stronger meaning for my friend than it did for me. I recognized the reminder its presence was for her of darker times.

I said nothing. I couldn't imagine how she must have felt as a child and teenager, not knowing if even the members of her own family could be trusted. Knowing that her every move on the street was being monitored. Knowing that acquaintances, neighbours, relatives could disappear without warning—sometimes they came back. Other times, they didn't.

"We didn't so much live in fear as we had an awareness that we were being monitored and that there were limits on our freedom. It wasn't a fear; fear is paralyzing. We weren't paralyzed with fear. We just lived with that awareness. That awareness was part of life."

The museum was housed in a dreary building with yellow linoleum on the floor, yellowed walls, and no windows. There was a display of cassette tapes that had been sent to East Germans from friends and relatives "on the other side" so that those behind the Iron Curtain could enjoy Western pop and rock music. The tapes that were confiscated were then used to record interrogation sessions.

Multiple objects on display had been used to spy on people, and it was all very James Bond-like. Buttons, pens, and briefcases with hidden cameras and/or microphones. Disguises that citizens used when spying on one another. Uniforms. Letters. (The Stasi read citizens' incoming mail.)

I had toured only about half of the museum, even though it was the size of a small house. I didn't want my curiosity about the macabre to traumatize my good friend even more than she already was. I had seen enough to get the gist of what the museum was all about. The person sitting beside me on that sidewalk—her body language, her silence—could tell me much more than the museum ever could.

During the Cold War, the Stasi had collected mountains of information on the people of East Germany. Every citizen had a file on them, and when the Wall came down, people were told they could look at their files.

But would I want to? Who would want to know that their uncle or son was spying on them for years?

Death Lives Here

A former co-worker of mine, Alex, was born in Munich and lived there until his parents moved their family of three to Canada when he was eleven years old. He asked me once, "Why are Canadians so fixated on and fascinated by World War II history and in particular, Germany's part in World War II?"

It's a great question, one that I don't necessarily have the answer to. After pondering for a few moments, I gave him *my* best answer, which is only from my perspective.

"Maybe it's because it's one of the most significant wars that Canada has been part of in the past century, and there are still people living who fought in it or had family members fighting in it. It's history but it's also within our lifetime, if you're talking about people who are old enough to have been alive during the war.

"I think also, at least for me, it's because there are so many of us here of German origin who either had family in Germany fighting against Canada or were German Canadians who were conscripted to fight for Canada, and the idea of fighting against your homeland presents a unique internal conflict. And if you're talking about genocide, the Holocaust hits home for Canadians of European descent more directly for those reasons than atrocities in other countries, such as Rwanda, because of the ancestral connections."

During that conversation, I relayed to him another moment of consideration for me that happened when Mom and I left Christine and Leipzig behind and continued on to Munich.

***

High on my to-do list for our trip to Germany was to visit a concentration camp, and I chose Dachau for its proximity to Munich. The town of Dachau and the Memorial Site of the former concentration camp are a short fifteen-kilometre train ride from Munich and easy to tour on a half-day trip.

Wine, Bach, and Cuckoo Clocks

Crossing those train tracks and walking through the gate under the sign "Arbeit Macht Frei" (work shall make you free) made my whole body shiver. I had brief flashbacks to the black and white movies my high school social studies teachers showed us—films of World War II battles and scenes, including clips and photos of prisoners under this sign, or the same one that hangs above the gate at Auschwitz. I was entering a world that I had studied as "history"—a place where atrocities had taken place but until that moment were only incidents in a history book or a film for me. I was about to experience that history: the buildings where these people were dehumanized—their identities taken away upon arrival—where they were tortured, where they worked, slept, cried, feared, and hoped.

Numerous visitors were walking around, but no one was speaking. No birds were chirping. The silence was eerie.

And the moment we passed through the gate and walked toward the office building where new prisoners who had disembarked from the train were taken and processed, I noticed a rank smell. It was a smell I had never experienced before. It was revolting, and though faint at times, it was constant. Once it hit me, I could smell it until we left the property.

We entered the first building, guided by our earphones, and heard how prisoners were directed from the train into this building, where they had to give their names and were stripped of their clothing and given ill-fitting prison uniforms. All of their body hair was shaved off and they were sent to the shower room in the next building to be disinfected.

It was during this tour that I learned more about the prisoners during World War II. Whether I had forgotten or simply not learned it, I was under the impression that all prisoners of Hitler's concentration camps were Jewish. His ant-Semitic views had been emphasized to me in my school courses, so while touring the camp, I was fascinated to learn that in addition to the Jewish people, a lot of the prisoners in Dachau were also Jehovah's Witnesses, Roma, homosexuals, and general criminals.

Dachau was one of the first camps Hitler established, one where the shower room was set up as a gas chamber (not all concentration camps had gas chambers). But more prisoners at Dachau died as a result of medical experiments and slave labour than being taken to the gas chamber for mass execution.

The audio tour guided us through the registration office and shower room to the buildings where the medical experiments took place and then to the dormitories. Between the shower room and the dormitory buildings is a wide, open area where other dormitories used to stand. Their prior existence is now only marked by wooden beams outlining where the foundations of the buildings were. This area looked similar to a large parking lot with the placings of the buildings marked out.

The sentinel towers still stood at each corner of the site, and as we made our way through the large open area where the dormitories used to stand and along the trenches that had been dug along the perimeter of the wall, we paused now and then. As I looked up to the towers, I imagined soldiers keeping guard with their rifles, looking down while prisoners worked or bunked down on the hard beds.

The last section of the property is across the barbed wire fence that circles the entire property and on the other side of the trenches, indicating that prisoners had likely been blocked from entering. In this area, at the end of a quiet, dirt path enveloped by trees and other greenery, the crematoriums stand. The area is peaceful, and anyone who didn't walk up close enough to see the ovens inside may think these buildings were small homes or tool sheds tucked away in someone's back yard adjacent to a welcoming park.

There weren't many people back in that area when Mom and I ventured that way. She and I stood in silence for a few moments looking at the ovens inside the small buildings.

Throughout our tour, the rancid, rank smell strengthened bit by bit. I couldn't think of what the source of the smell could be. I have never smelled a rotting human corpse; growing up on a farm, there were times I would encounter a rotting animal in the field, but the smell at Dachau was stauncher and rottener than anything like that. Surely after all of these years, there would be no linger of the smell of human corpses? I still don't know what the smell was, and when I returned to Dachau several years later with friends who wanted to visit the site, the smell wasn't there. That day, when Mom and I were there, I named it in my mind The Smell of Death, as I couldn't attach it to anything else.

Wine, Bach, and Cuckoo Clocks

By the time we boarded the train back to Munich, the smell had planted itself in my throat, and the thought of eating anything for dinner that night repulsed me. I could now taste the smell; I wondered how long it would be until I could no longer smell, taste, or even remember this nastiness.

As I sat on the train with my face in a bit of a scowl because of the smell, I asked my mom, "Is it just me or did you smell that, too?"

She confirmed that the smell was not simply a product of my imagination; she had smelled and was now tasting it too.

We sat in silence on the train for a few more moments before I spoke again. It wasn't like her to look so somber and to be so silent, so I asked, "Is something wrong?"

She paused a moment before answering.

"I had no idea anything like that had ever happened."

"What do you mean?" I asked.

"What happened to all of those people there. I never knew that places like this existed."

"What?! But we learned all of this in high school!"

"You did," she replied, "but I didn't. Remember, I went to high school in the 1950s. World War II had just ended. It wasn't history yet, so we didn't study it in history class.

"Plus, remember, your grandparents and great-grandparents are German. We never talked about the war."

It was my turn to pull in my breath and process this information. It had never occurred to me that my mother's generation wouldn't have learned about the Holocaust in school. I was struck, at that moment, at how shocking it must have been for her to learn for the first time about the true extent of these atrocities—to see, in front of her, evidence of what I heard learned two decades prior. I had also never thought much about what it must have been like to have been German/of German heritage in Canada during that time.

My memory flashed back to several years earlier when Mom had taken my sister and me to see *The Diary of Anne Frank* at a local dinner theatre. During the intermission, we remained in our seats and at one point, Mom blurted out, with no warning, "We have relatives in South America, you know."

"What?!" my sister said.

"Yeah, they moved there from Germany after World War II," Mom replied.

"GAH! I don't want to hear about this!" I said. I knew that a lot of Nazis had fled Germany at the end of World War II and relocated to South America so as to escape prosecution. I assumed her comment meant that we had extended family members who fit into this category. I didn't want to know if that's what she was implying.

We changed the subject. I never asked or learned more about this tidbit of information.

On the train from Dachau to Munich, I also thought about Heidi, a former co-worker in Calgary whose father had been part of the Hitler Youth before immigrating to Canada after World War II. He apparently told her and her sister this much but consistently refused to say more. She said he would get angry if pressed to disclose any details.

"We don't talk about it," is what everybody says. Nobody talks about it.

The rest of the short train ride was silent.

***

As the day continued, the smell and taste of death in our throats dissipated, and by evening, we were ready for a good meal. To lighten the mood after our visit to Dachau, I took Mom to one of the places in Munich I had put high on my list of places to visit.

Munich's Hofbräuhaus is a 16th-century beer hall/restaurant offering an Oktoberfest atmosphere any day of the year, any time of the day. Visitors can go at eleven in the morning and be met with the same heavy food, drink, and live rocking tuba and accordion music as they would at 11 pm. It's a lively place where visitors can order a huge meal of pork knuckle and Spätzle (small noodles the shape and size of a large raisin), down a massive one-litre stein of beer (or two), and meet fellow travellers from around the world.

I couldn't get Mom to dance to the polka music at the Hofbräuhaus, but we both ordered and ate a massive meal of pork knuckle, potato dumplings, and cabbage. My mom would claw her way out of her grave and scold me if I failed to mention that the yellow liquid in her beer stein was actually Apfelschorle—sparking apple juice—and not beer. Mine was certainly the latter.

The Best and Wurst of Nuremberg

Like so many of Germany's cities, Nuremberg was heavily bombed during World War II and as a result, much of the city has been rebuilt. Unique to Nuremberg, however, is the fact that much of the city's art was protected during the bombing because it was moved and stashed in the city's underground cellars beneath Nuremberg Castle. Among the treasures that were stored in the cellars were stained glass windows from various churches around town, furniture, carvings, and sculptures.

We didn't tour the art bunker, but I did drag Mom into another part of underground Nuremberg: the medieval dungeons directly under city hall. Mom would have never chosen to see these dungeons, but she had deferred to me to plan everything we were doing.

I'm fascinated by the dark side of humanity and have always been interested in the history of torture. How and why humans can be so awful to one another intrigues me. I feel guilty when I squash a spider—I can't imagine even punching another human much less torturing or killing someone. But I'm eager to learn about the psychology and motivation behind the evil acts humans have done to one another throughout history.

The self-guided tour of the dungeons took us past the cells where prisoners were held as they were waiting to be tried for their crimes. Various sharp and pointy torture instruments—tools used for stretching or choking—were on the walls as well as shackles that would have restrained the prisoners. If they denied the charges against them, prisoners were tortured in hopes that they would confess.

After visiting the dungeons, our first stop on the World War II history part of our tour around Nuremberg was to Die Kongresshalle (The Congress Hall), which was intended to be a massive Nazi rally centre. Work began on it in 1935, but construction was never completed. The shape and style of the building is reminiscent of the Roman Colosseum; it is a horseshoe-shaped building that holds the Nuremberg Documentation Center—a museum depicting how the

Nazis used propaganda during their regime—and the exhibition of Faszination und Gewalt (fascination and terror) in the north wing. The displays in this building focus on the origins and evolution of the Nazi party: how Hitler came to power and how he held on to it as long as he did. The purpose of the display is to educate in hopes that such a leader can never rise to power again.

Our touring for the day ended at Zeppelinfeld, the large open-air square adjacent to The Congress Hall. This open field is where crowds of thousands would gather and listen to Hitler's speeches. At the front of Zeppelinfeld, on the stairs where Hitler would have stood, I had to look around for a few minutes, taking in yet another site I had only seen in black and white pictures and film images prior to setting foot there. I spent a few moments matching the images from my memory to what I was seeing in front of me. I had the same sense here as I did when I was standing in Tiananmen Square a few years prior—the same need to pause, reflect, and allow my brain to connect its historic images with my present reality.

Nuremburg is known not only for its World War II sites and the trials that took place after the war but also for its sausage and Lebkuchen (gingerbread cookies).

In the evening, we looked for a place for dinner. Sausage was on both of our minds since Nuremburg boasts of its own style of Wurst.

> To qualify as a Nuremberg sausage, the sausage must be no longer than nine centimetres and weigh no more than 25 grams. Nuremberg bratwurst contain mace, pepper, and marjoram in a recipe that dates back to the city's heyday as a medieval trading town. A Würstlein, or sausage supervisor, was appointed in 1315.[6]

The Nuremburg Sausage Protection Association is surely dead serious about its city's Wurst being the best.

The restaurant we went to had no lack of German options on the menu, and as was the case with most places, they had an English version of their menu. Mom and I placed our order.

Our server brought us a basket of bread. German bread is fresh, soft, and flavourful, and there is always a wide variety of delicious choices at any meal or in any bakery. This basket contained eight different types of rolls, bread sticks, pretzels, and slices of bread.

Mom and I each munched on a couple of pieces of bread while waiting for our meals. When our orders arrived, we eagerly downed them. The famed sausages were the size and shape of breakfast sausages and were a dark colour. The herbs and spices in them made for several tasty bites. The best sausage I'd ever had was made by my parents, grandparents, and the German men at my hometown's Lutheran church for Shrove Tuesday. The prized Nuremberg sausages jumped to the top of the list with them.

Our server took the bread basket away as she was clearing our sausage-and-sauerkraut plates, and shortly thereafter brought our bill. Mom and I were both confused.

"What's this extra charge?" Mom asked me.

I didn't know what it was for so when the server returned, I asked.

"The bread," she said.

Neither of us had had any idea that the bread wasn't complimentary. We hadn't ordered it, so we assumed it was free.

This surprise brought to mind a funny incident I had when I was teaching ESL in Calgary (the same school where I taught Christine). A few of us on staff were in Banff one weekend, escorting a student group around the town and surrounding areas. We were staying at the hostel and spent the weekend hiking, wandering around town, and enjoying the hot springs. On the evening that we were staying over, our group went to a pub for dinner.

Several minutes after placing our order, we received our drinks. While we were waiting for our food, one of the German-speaking students from Switzerland piped up:

"Loh-na. When do we become bread?" he asked me.

I suppressed a giggle because, having studied German, I knew what he meant.

The word bekommen in German means receive, and it is pronounced similar to bay-comen. Poor Mattias had mixed up his English with German.

"Some restaurants bring bread before the meal, but pubs usually don't. I don't expect they will bring us any bread," I told him.

Wine, Bach, and Cuckoo Clocks

Our sausage meal in Nuremberg, albeit delectable, was a little greasy. My stomach is made of iron and although I have had food poisoning a couple of times, it takes a lot to make me sick from something I ate. That sausage, however, did send me running to the bathroom to sit on the toilet a couple of times before we went to sleep.

The next morning, I was up before my mom, which was unheard of. (To me, morning doesn't start until the clock shows double digits.)

As I was getting ready, Mom said, "I need a break. You go explore without me. I'll stay back and rest."

My mom was prone to migraines, but that wasn't what was ailing her. I assumed it was a combo of the greasy sausage, since her stomach was much more sensitive than mine, and her need for a break from all of the gloom and doom of the World War II sites I had been guiding her to. Maybe the torture implements in the dungeons had put her over the edge. I figured she needed a few hours to get happy and let her stomach settle.

When I returned later in the day, Mom assured me that she was feeling rested up and was ready to find something for dinner.

"Not sausage, though, please," she requested.

***

Before going on our trip, I had riffled through Mom's family history documents and found the name of a town near Stuttgart where many members of my mom's family originated. We stopped there, in Heilbronn, for a couple of days on our way back to Frankfurt from Munich. Heilbronn is a small town that international tourists would have no reason to visit.

By this time, I was feeling quite confident in my limited German, but the young man working at the hotel desk pegged us right away as foreigners and greeted us warmly in English.

"You are here for two nights?" he asked.

"Yes," I replied. "The reservation is under the name 'Stuber.'"

"But our wine festival was one week ago," the clerk informed us. "Why are you here?"

I burst out laughing, and he laughed along. Apparently they didn't get many international visitors in this obscure little town.

Why *were* we there? Heilbronn is a town name that appears several times in my Mom's family history documents. I had told her I wanted to visit the town because I wanted to see where her family was from.

It was a quiet, small place that was one of my favourite towns on our trip, full of half-timbered houses with yellow, blue, and red flowers filling window boxes. A small river ran through the town, and parks along the river were lush with trees and bright green grass. Even the bridge over the river was picturesque. We spent most of our time walking, exploring the town, and seeking out and wandering through every cemetery in town in a futile search for headstones that would confirm my ancestors were from here.

Our last day in Heilbronn was my birthday. The next day was going to be a travel day to Frankfurt followed by an early morning flight back to Calgary. It seemed fitting to be celebrating my birthday in the town of our ancestors and on the last full touring day of our vacation. As had been the case throughout our entire trip, I scouted out a restaurant where we could enjoy German food and wine. It was our last chance to indulge in the local fare, and on my birthday in particular, I wanted one last feast of the meats and doughy stuff I love so much.

As we were poring over the menu, I noticed there was an entire section titled "Offal." Having grown up on a cattle ranch and having helped my parents butcher chickens, turkeys, cattle, and pigs throughout my childhood, I am not at all squeamish when it comes to eating chicken feet, heart and liver from chickens or bovine, or chicken gizzards (chickens have gizzards instead of stomachs). In fact, my sister and I used to fight over the chicken hearts unless we were willing to cut them in half. Gizzards were one of my favourite treats when we had fried home-grown chicken. And I took cold beef tongue sandwiches to school on many occasions. Fortunately for sibling harmony, chickens have two feet, so we didn't have to fight over those.

However, here in Germany was an additional menu item available that I had never eaten before; it had in fact, never occurred to me to eat this part of the cow. Udder. Yep, the large bag-shaped organ on a cow that holds the milk and has four long, finger-shaped nipples or teats. Cow boob. At first I wasn't sure I was reading the menu correctly but yes, cow udder was listed. It sounded ... "udderly" unappealing. I pointed it out to my mom, and she suggested, "We could order that and turn it upside down, and that can be your birthday cake!"

I ordered the Schnitzel.

***

Two years after I went to Germany with Mom, I found out that I was half right about her not feeling well in Nuremberg. Her needing to rest was because of the sausage. But not because it was simply a meal that didn't agree with her. Her stomach issues that day were the first symptoms of a serious health issue. After being told on multiple occasions for over a year after our trip that she had a bladder infection and then that she had polyps in her colon, my mom was diagnosed with pancreatic cancer. Several months after her diagnosis, she finally told me, "That day in Germany was the day I realized something was terribly wrong." She had been feeling unwell off and on for several months prior but of course she never complained. She knew deep down whatever was ailing her was more serious than a bladder infection, but as pancreatic cancer tends to be elusive, it was almost two years before the golf-ball-sized tumour showed up on a scan.

True to form, my mom remained stoic throughout her diagnosis and subsequent two-year battle with pancreatic cancer. I never saw her cry once during that time. I've inherited a lot of traits from my mother, one of them being my stoic nature; I bawled like an angry baby when I left the doctor's office the day she got the diagnosis, but other than that, and to this day, I have not cried about my mother's horrible last two years and ultimate death.

I will forever be grateful that we went on that trip, as it was the last vacation she took before she died a few years later.

The Stüber Hotel

My second visit to Germany in 2008, two years after Mom and I had gone, was with friends. Sher is sixteen years my senior, and we have a similar background, both having grown up on farms in central Alberta. Many of our family traditions are the same or similar as she also has German ancestry.

Sher and her husband swear by Rick Steves's travel books. After they had gotten their hands on his travel guide for Germany, we got together for dinner at their house one night six weeks before our trip to do some planning.

As we were enjoying our dessert and coffee, Richard pulled out the book and started telling me some of the places they had researched. Yes, we needed to see the main sites in Munich, and being wine drinkers, they definitely wanted to enjoy some good German wine. I assured them that the wine would be available anywhere but particularly in the Rhein Valley. And so Richard flipped to the Rhein section of the book.

"Oh my God!" he exclaimed. "Listen to this!"

He read aloud the description of a wonderful-sounding hotel along the banks of the Rhein River in a small town called Bacharach. Bacharach was surrounded by hills that were covered with vineyards.

"And the owner of this place, the Rhein Hotel, is Andreas Stüber! Are you related to him?" he asked me. (Andreas's last name has the umlaut over the u; I'm not 100 percent sure, but I believe my last name had the umlaut on it originally but somewhere along the way, it was eliminated so as to fit into English-speaking Canada.)

"What?! Let me see that!"

Richard liked to tease me so for all I knew, he was making this up to make fun of me because I was always going on about my German heritage.

But nope. There it was: Andreas Stüber. Rhein Hotel. Bacharach, Germany. The heart of wine country.

I had no idea if I was related to this Andreas Stüber or not. I knew my last name isn't common, even in Germany, so there was a good chance I was related to him at least distantly.

The three of us decided we needed to go there for the wine, the scenery, but especially because of the owner's name. The guidebook indicated that the hotel was small but had a few rooms. Richard brought out the laptop and went onto the hotel's website.

"They have a two-bedroom option. We could book that," he said, showing me the screen.

Perfect! Richard and Sher could have the bigger room, if there was a size difference, and I would take the smaller. He reserved the room and booked a rental car for our two-week vacation.

***

The car wasn't big, of course; this was Europe. Everything in Canada and the US is so much bigger than in many other parts of the world: houses, cars, meals. The car was a compact four-door with a hatchback, so we stuffed our suitcases into the cargo area with another bag or two plopped in the back seat, and I helped jump on the bags to squash them enough that we could close the door. As I squeezed myself into the back seat, I remembered the joke, "This is what ten pounds of jelly looks like in a five-pound bag!"

In our planning, we had also failed to consider that unlike in Canada and the US, the rest of the world favours stick shifts, so Richard was designated to do most of the driving. I offered to pitch in now and then if he needed a rest and if we were on flat, open roads since my ability to shift gears is inferior even on said flat, open roads.

Once we got on the highway with Richard behind the wheel, Sher pulled out the Garmin GPS that they had brought from home. But we had also failed to recognize that the GPS, which they had purchased in Calgary, was going to be vocalizing the German place names with a standard North American accent. Therefore, German words like Strasse (street), were barked at us not with proper German pronunciation (straw-seh) but with an American twang: straaaaaas (rhyming with ass). When Sher programmed in Bacharach, we quickly found humorous the horrible pronunciation of the town's name as batch-a-ratch. We giggled every time the GPS directed us on the slightly-more-than-an-hour drive from Frankfurt.

We found Bacharach, and as the guidebook promised, it was a quiet town on the banks of the Rhein River, surrounded by hilly vineyards. Castles lined the riverbanks in the distance. The Rhein Hotel was along the river, and Richard pulled up in front of the garage door. The hotel looked more like a large three-storey house than a hotel. Obviously it was a family-run place with a few guest rooms.

When we started climbing the steps to the entrance and announced our arrival, a young man descended to open the garage door and usher Richard in. We left the car in the garage for the duration of our stay since Bacharach was so small (population around 1,500) that anything we wanted to see and do was easily accessible on foot.

Richard had reserved the room under his name, so until our cheerful arrival, the owners and staff had had no idea that another Stuber was coming to stay there.

"This is Lorna Stuber," Sher said to the woman checking us in as she put her arm around me. "We're from Canada. You may be related to each other."

The young woman smiled and said, "Perhaps."

"Do you have family in Canada?" I asked.

"I don't know. My sister is studying in the US, in California."

"I have no idea if we are related to each other," I said. "Maybe we are, but I don't know much about my father's family connections here in Germany."

The young woman gave us our key and showed us to our room on the top floor.

"Here is your room. There are towels, and if you need anything, please let us know! Enjoy your stay!" she said and then walked away.

We stepped into the room. Paused. Looked at each other. And burst out laughing.

Our "two-bedroom" booking was a room with two beds. Not two bedrooms, but a single bed along the wall right inside the door and a double bed across from that. The bathroom was directly across from the doorway. There was plenty of room on the side for our suitcases, but we were a little stunned at having to share a room: me, my friend, and her husband.

Wine, Bach, and Cuckoo Clocks

Ah, well. We shrugged it off and settled in. Whether it was because we had no choice, because we were all good friends, or because Bacharach was wine country, and we certainly sampled our share of the local product as early as the first evening, we were all comfortable enough with each other and the two-bed room arrangement to the point that Richard was walking around the room that evening in only his underwear while Sher and I continued to laugh at the misunderstanding.

***

The Rhein Hotel and town of Bacharach are hidden gems in the Rhein Valley, west and a little south of Frankfurt. Christine, who has lived in the former East Germany for most of her life, had never heard of the town. Steps from the hotel is the shore of the river, with benches scattered about, where visitors can relax and take in the scenery. We saw that full- and half-day cruises were available down the Rhein, so we booked ourselves on a half-day cruise, viewing the castles along the shore while enjoying some of the local wines. The Loreley Rock, a UNESCO World Heritage Site, is a short distance down the river from Bacharach. Clemens Brentano was so inspired by the Loreley cliffs that in 1801, he wrote his poem "Lore Lay" about a beautiful woman who was adored by many men. The legend of Lore Lay says that she was suffering from unrequited love for a man, so she wished to die. She supposedly caused other men their deaths by bewitching them so she was brought before a bishop for penance. Instead of convicting her for using magic, the bishop too was enchanted by her beauty and sent her to a nunnery to atone for her sins. On the way, she and the three knights guarding her passed the 132-metre-high rock beside the Rhein. Lore Lay asked to climb it to watch out for her unfaithful lover one last time. She believed she spotted him on a ship and fell to her death. The rock now bears her name.

The three of us were surprised at how many castles were perched along the shores of the river. The day we chose was warm, breezy, and sunny. A perfect day to be out on the water in the sunshine, enjoying the scenery with a full wine glass in hand the whole time.

The Stüber Hotel

***

The main street of Bacharach is around the corner from the hotel, and a walk in each direction down the main street offers up touristy shops, bakeries, wine Stubes (a Stube is like a pub), and various other shops. Many of the wine Stubes offer flights so that visitors can sample several local wines without getting too inebriated.

Richard, Sher, and I visited a wine Stube two blocks down from our hotel and were deep into tasting our wine flights when we saw Andreas walk in and talk to someone who we assumed to be the Stube owner. There is something comforting and enjoyable about the universal small-town feeling of seeing the same people on the street day to day and observing the locals interact with each other. The two men were obviously friends but also likely business associates as Andreas, the chef at his hotel's restaurant, was probably placing a wine order or talking about stock for his restaurant. We enjoyed the wine enough that we bought a case on our way out that evening. We were at the beginning of our two-week trip. We had yet to make our way to Leipzig to visit Christine, and we were planning a three-day drive through the Black Forest and southern Germany. We figured we could pick up some of the delicious bread and deli meats available everywhere in Germany and picnic somewhere in the Black Forest. We also expected to have enough wine left at the end of our trip to each take a bottle home.

As we were wandering around town the next day, taking in the shopping and adoring the cobblestone streets, shops, and local libations, Sher and I, being high school English teachers, were distracted by a poster on a bulletin board on the one of the shops. We saw the word Othello and moved closer to look at the details. Of course the poster was entirely in German, but between my rudimentary ability to understand the language and the fact that it was mostly a visual poster, we determined that some local group was putting on performances of *Othello*. We deduced that the performance was to be held on certain dates, including that evening, in the courtyard of the town's castle, which is now a youth hostel. Richard was outnumbered: two English teachers versus a plumber. But he was always game for live theatre, so we decided to take in that evening's performance.

Wine, Bach, and Cuckoo Clocks

We had hiked up to the castle the previous day to do some exploring and see how high we could get. The hike was short but worth it as the castle grounds were green and well-kept, and the green hills overlooking the Rhein Valley were chock full of rows of grapevines lining the hiking trail on one side. We got a bit farther than the castle, which was at the top of the mountain, but beyond the castle was a walking path that ran along some more vineyards. The vines were heavy with grapes, and we wandered for an hour, taking in the fresh, warm air in the green, lush wine country.

The night of the play, we trekked back up to the castle, a small plastic bag in my hand, filled with our snacks: a bottle of Rhein Riesling and several fresh pretzels. A crowd was beginning to form as we got to the castle. We settled onto a cement bench in the courtyard.

The play was, of course, in German, but Sher and I had taught *Othello* several times throughout our careers, so we had no problem understanding what was going on.

Weather speaks a universal language, so the German lines of the play did not prevent us from understanding halfway through the play that we were going to get soaked. Storm clouds had rolled in during Act I, and the rain started to sprinkle down. The actors soldiered on, so we remained in our seats, enjoying the performance, our wine, and the increasingly-soggy pretzels. We were a little miffed about our wine getting watered down, and the soggier the pretzels got as we munched on them, the less appealing they got, but we remained ...

... until the clouds opened up into a deluge so quickly that everyone was caught off guard. Within moments, we were soaked, and the remains of our pretzels were beyond rescue. The actors called off the performance before everyone had a chance to die in Act 2. (SPOILER ALERT: almost everybody dies in Shakespeare's tragedies, including *Othello*.)

We schlepped back down the mountain, giggling and shrugging at how wet we were. It was, after all, a summer evening. We were on holiday in a foreign country, and a little rainwater on the hair and pretzels was only a minor annoyance.

***

When I was working on the first draft of this book, a wonderful opportunity arose. Three years prior, I had friended Mr. Ghidina, my junior high school science teacher, on Facebook. After not having seen or had any contact with each other for more than thirty years, we struck up several private chats on Messenger to catch up and reconnect. He was obviously still the same gregarious, fun-loving Italian-Canadian man he had been when I was his adoring student. He had been living in Calgary for a couple of decades at this point, and I had been living in Calgary or its suburbs for almost thirty years, so we made a promise that as soon as COVID restrictions allowed, we would get together for coffee or lunch.

In September 2022, we were able to meet for lunch. We spent an hour-and-a-half chatting, laughing, catching up, and eating great Italian food. I found myself wishing I could stay another hour or more to continue the great conversation. But we made a promise we would again meet for lunch sometime soon.

One of our main topics of conversation was our mutual love of travel: how incredible Italy is, how much we both wanted to travel to Israel and Jordan, and how much we both loved Germany.

"Yeah, everyone thinks Germans are so serious and stuffy," I said, "but they're not. I can tell I'm German because whenever I'm in Germany, I find the locals have the same dry, witty sense of humour as I do, and I feel like I belong there. German people are welcoming and friendly and funny."

"They are. We only went to three places in Germany, and they were all completely different, but we loved all three cities," he replied.

"Where did you go?" I asked.

"Berlin, Munich, and Bacharach."

I shrieked and burst out laughing—and my laugh ain't soft and quiet. Everyone in the restaurant turned and looked at me.

He seemed a little embarrassed and caught off guard at my reaction.

"Why are you laughing so hard?" he asked.

"Bacharach! Really?" I asked.

"Yeah."

"That's so funny! My friend Christine, who lives in Leipzig, had never heard of Bacharach until I visited her after spending a few days

Wine, Bach, and Cuckoo Clocks

there. I mean, she's German. She's lived in Germany almost all of her life, and she'd never heard of Bacharach. It's so funny and random that you went there as one of your stops! Why Bacharach of all places?"

I started to think I sounded like the fellow who worked at the hotel that Mom and I had stayed at in Heilbronn, asking us, "Why are you here?!"

"We wanted to go to the Rhein because it's wine country, and Bacharach is right along the river."

"Did you stay at the Stuber Hotel?" I laughed.

He had no idea what I was talking about.

"It's actually called the Rhein Hotel and is just steps from the river," I said.

"Ah, no. We stayed at a hotel further into the town."

"I call it the Stuber Hotel because the owners are named Stüber. I have no idea if I'm related to them or not, but when my friends and I were planning a trip to Germany together, they read about this place in Rick Steves's Germany guidebook. When we saw the owners were named Stüber, that was the deciding factor. We had to stay there."

He laughed. "We enjoyed our time in Bacharach."

"Yeah, it's such a pretty area," I agreed. "And great wine."

Several months after this lunch meeting, I was in a meeting of a local board I was serving on in my town. One of the board members, a mild-mannered, well-dressed, mostly bald gentleman, had returned two weeks prior from a trip to Germany with his wife.

"Funny story!" he said, looking at me, before we started the meeting.

"Yes?"

"One of the places we stayed in Germany was a town called Bacharach."

"WHAT?" I laughed. "Really?"

I couldn't wait to hear what he was going to say next.

"Yes, and when we were walking along the street, we saw a sign for a barber shop. The sign had your last name on it."

"So did you go in for a trim and tell them you know one of their Canadian relatives?" I teased him.

***

The Stüber Hotel

From Bacharach, Richard, Sher, and I went south. We were ultimately headed for Munich, but we had several items on our to-do list along the way:

- stop in Baden-Baden to enjoy the public spa baths
- take a drive through the Black Forest, thereby taking "the scenic route" to Munich
- enjoy a picnic in the Black Forest
- stop to see the World's Largest Cuckoo Clock in Triberg, deep in the heart of the Black Forest

Baden-Baden is known for its public baths, discovered more than 2,000 years ago by the Romans and renowned for their healing qualities. The town is appropriately named because baden is the German verb for bathe/take a bath or swim. The thermal springs running under the city are the source of the most mineral-rich water in Germany, and the water is used not only in the baths but also for drinking and inhaling. The baths in Baden-Baden provide multiple options for those wanting to benefit from the mineral water. There are baths for nude bathing, in true Roman style, and opportunities for aromatherapy, yoga, and soaking in the salt waters of the Salina Sea Salt Grotto, where salts from the Dead Sea and the Himalayas are pumped through the ventilation system for healing respiratory ailments.

The city, on the east bank of the Rhein River, is in the mountainous and forest regions of the Black Forest, so in addition to the spas it is famous for, the area is also scenic.

Since Richard had been doing all of the driving up to this point, I offered to switch off with him. I wasn't great at driving a stick-shift, so I started in Bacharach but planned to pull over shortly before we got to Baden-Baden so that he could drive in the city. However, the town snuck up on us, and before I knew it, I was driving in the town with nowhere to pull over. I decided I was getting more comfortable with switching the gears so I would finish driving at our hotel.

Sher had punched the address of the hotel into the GPS, and I was following the audio directions, glancing now and then at the map on the GPS. I was fairly accustomed to most of the street signs in Germany, some of which are a little different than the ones in Canada, but at one point, by the time I realized that the sign I had just passed indicated that the street to my left was a pedestrian zone only, it was too late; I had already turned.

The street was too narrow for me to turn around. I was terrified to throw the car into reverse, so I inched the car forward, drawing a few glances and glares, but I made sure I was driving so slowly that no one was in danger.

Until I saw a bit of a hurdle in front of me. Two restaurants, one on each side of the street, had tables set up for outdoor dining, and the tables were full. There wasn't enough room ahead of me for a car to pass through, which made sense since the street was a pedestrian zone. They wouldn't have thought they needed to space the tables apart far enough for a car to pass by.

Fortunately, an older gentlemen saw our car coming straight toward them, albeit slowly enough to stop, but I didn't need to stop. He stood on the side of the street directing others to move their tables, move themselves, and watch out for me as he waved me on through. I was mortified but I couldn't help bursting out in laughter. Sher followed suit, and Richard, in the back seat, teased me, "Geez, Lorna, where did you learn how to drive?!"

I was happy to turn left again and get the heck off the street, venturing onto more unknown streets but knowing from the GPS that we were getting closer to our hotel. Relief was in sight.

Until I turned onto another narrow street. There were no restaurants or even people on this one, but the road was a dead end. It was blocked off for construction.

No matter. I'll just take a turn down another street and the GPS will recalculate for me.

And it did. I took a bit of a detour, and a couple minutes later, the GPS directed me back in the right general direction ... and directly back to the construction site I had just veered away from.

And so I turned in a different direction and turned again.

And drove up to the exact same damn construction site for a third time. Our hotel was within a few hundred metres, and it was starting to appear that the only way to get to the hotel was through this construction site. But I couldn't pass through it; it was blocked off, and even if it hadn't been, I didn't want to risk damaging the car.

I took a longer detour on my fourth attempt and at last, found success. No more pylons, no more pedestrians dining with my exhaust fumes enhancing the flavour of their meals.

***

The next morning, we got up and spent a leisurely morning having coffee and breakfast before going out in search of the baths. We figured spending the day at the spa enjoying a relaxing soak would be lovely. We would end the day with a nice dinner and then resume our journey the next morning.

Richard took the wheel and got us to the baths without driving through any outdoor cafes or construction zones.

This was the one part of the trip for which none of us had done a ton of research. We have hot springs in Banff, near where I live; there are lots of them in British Columbia—indoor and outdoor—and the three of us had also all been to the spa in Moose Jaw, Saskatchewan, on separate occasions, so we were looking forward to enjoying the warm, comforting mineral water of this town.

As we approached the front door, we saw signage that indicated "This way to the nude baths."

Um, what?

We had just come from Bacharach, where we had shared a hotel room, but this was a bit of a higher level of familiarity than walking around a hotel room in our underwear in front of each other. I mulled over our situation for a second, and Sher and I looked at each other.

"No way," Richard stated as we stood there, still pondering this predicament.

"Well, we could always take turns," I offered. "You guys can go first, and I can wait, or … something?" I was trying to come up with a creative solution to the fact that we had driven all this way for perhaps nothing, when we saw some other people enter the building with their bathing suits in hand.

"Wait, what?" Sher and I chimed in at the same time. We looked more closely at the signage, which included a map.

"Ah, there *is* a section where don't have to be nude."

Wine, Bach, and Cuckoo Clocks

The section for those in bathing suits was quite large; there were different pools of different temperatures, and once in that area, patrons could switch back and forth between the pools.

We spent a couple hours in the baths in an atmosphere that didn't push our friendship farther past any limits that had been left behind in the hotel room in Bacharach.

A Little Cuckoo

When I was a kid, one of the reasons I enjoyed going to Grandma and Grandpa Stuber's house, besides getting to eat my grandma's delectable German-style cooking and spend time with my grandparents of course, was because they had a cuckoo clock in their living room. I was only three or four years old when I clued in to the fact that when the longest hand on the clock reached the twelve, a tiny bird would come out and sing a funny song. Every time we arrived at my grandparents' place for a visit, I would rush into the living room to see how far away from the twelve the hand was and make sure I made it back to the living room in time to catch this enchanting performance.

Sher and I, both being of German ancestry, felt we had no choice but to witness the mesmerizing performance of Triberg's world famous cuckoo bird emerging from his little house to sing a little song. After all, if this were indeed *the* largest cuckoo clock in the world, we certainly could not come this close without witnessing this wondrous demonstration.

We left Baden-Baden with our suitcases jammed into our little rental car. And now that we had loaded up on a case of wine, we would certainly have no choice but to drink some of it so as to ease up the load on the car. As we reached the northern edge of the Black Forest, we stopped to pick up some pastries, bread, sandwich meats, chocolate, chips, and other drinks to fill out our picnic options (up to that point we only had the wine). One item that caught my eye was turkey-and-stuffing-flavoured potato chips. Who doesn't love Christmas dinner with all the trimmings? And here it was, in a bag, in potato-chip form! I had to try them. And since we were driving through the Black Forest, we also felt we must pick up three pieces of Black Forest cake.

After paying for our purchases and while walking back to the car, we paused to watch the baker pulling loaves of bread from the outdoor stone oven and putting more in.

"Mmm, I bet his bread is good," I said.

We watched the baker for a few moments and then wedged ourselves back into the car. With Richard at the wheel, we went south.

The Black Forest was exactly how I had envisioned the Sherwood Forest when I was a child hearing the stories of Robin Hood and his merry men. To me, Robin Hood's homeland was similar to the forests of other children's stories, particularly fairy tales, and then later the images I had in my mind of Birnam Wood in *Macbeth*. It may be as simple as having never been to Europe until my late twenties, but my image of all of these forests and woods in Europe was quite similar to each other and different to the forests of the Rocky Mountains. The trees of the Black Forest are tall, thin, and plentiful. And the trees seemed darker than ours at home. Our view also revealed dense thick forest with a bit of an eerie atmosphere, perhaps because of the influence of all the big bad wolves and other villains I had read about while forming my initial images of European forests. It was also rainy and foggy off and on all day.

A couple of hours into our drive, we decided to find a good spot to pull over for lunch. There were no towns along our route, nor had we seen any roadside rest areas, but we did find a spot where we could pull off the highway and park safely away from other traffic. As luck would have it, we came across this pullout at a time when the sun peeked out from behind the clouds and the mist.

We discovered that we had forgotten one vital ingredient in our picnic basket: cups to drink the wine from. We had nothing we could use, but since we'd just spent three days walking around the same hotel room in our dainties, we figured we were good enough friends that we could drink out of the same bottle. Sher screwed the cap off the wine and we passed the bottle around as if we were sharing a joint. I have a terrific picture of Sher, who is five foot nothing, head bent all the way back, swigging the last of the wine from the bottle.

We made sandwiches (we had had the foresight to buy some great German mustard to put on our bread and deli meat concoctions) and devoured the token Black Forest cake. We did have plastic forks, so although we didn't have plates, we were able to eat our dessert without creating much of a mess, noting how clever we were to be eating Black

Forest cake in the *middle* of the Black Forest. We packed up our garbage and resumed our drive.

Another hour and a bit into our drive to Triberg, I decided it was time to try the turkey-and-stuffing-flavoured potato chips.

I opened the bag and poked my nose inside.

"Oh my God, this smells exactly like Christmas dinner!" I said.

"See?" I thrust the bag into the front seat for Sher to smell it.

"Oh my God, you're right!"

"Take some," I told her while she was holding the bag.

She grabbed a handful and passed the bag back to me.

I tried one.

"They *taste* exactly like Christmas dinner!"

The flavour wasn't as fake and weird as I had feared it might be. It tasted exactly like turkey and stuffing. In potato-chip form.

I sat in the back seat like a little kid, crunching away on the chips, pushing the bag into the gap between the front seats now and then so Sher and Richard could have their share. It didn't take us long to finish off 90 percent of the bag. I put the rest aside for later.

Half an hour after finishing off our Christmas-dinner-in-chip-form, my stomach started feeling a tiny bit awful. I chalked it up to having gas. Maybe I'd have to request a bathroom stop before long.

Nope. Within moments I started feeling somewhat awful.

Hmmm. What's going on? Was it something I ate?

The whipped cream on the Black Forest cake was fresh.

The wine? We had shared a bottle between the three of us and on a full stomach, so it wasn't a matter of too much alcohol on an empty stomach. The deli meats and bread were all fresh. Weird.

I opened up the chip bag again, peering in to look at the six or seven remaining chips. All of a sudden, I felt *really* awful; the smell of the chips caused my stomach to lurch—not enough to throw up, but enough to snap the bag shut again and shove it as far away from me as possible.

It was the chips. Not only had my stomach's reaction screamed that to me loud and clear, but this time, when I opened the bag, I didn't smell the wonderful aroma of turkey and stuffing and sage and parsley and deliciousness; I smelled chemicals. The fake, revolting, stomach-churning smell of fake food flavoured by potentially toxic substances.

Wine, Bach, and Cuckoo Clocks

My mouth was salivating so I knew I was getting close to barfing. I debated asking Richard to pull over. I took a drink of water, and that settled my stomach a bit, but then I started to sweat. I sipped more water off and on for a minute.

Should I ask or should I wait?

I didn't want to wait until it was too late and he was unable to pull over lest I have to throw up in the car, but I wasn't convinced that I needed to throw up. I opened the car window to get some fresh air, and I kept drinking water.

Eventually, my stomach settled, and I remained silent and well-behaved until we got to Triberg.

By the time we arrived, heavy fog had settled in and rain was pounding down, so we ran from the car into the massive gift shop that was in the building that housed THE WORLD'S LARGEST CUCKOO CLOCK. (Note: There seems to be a bit of a controversy as to who has the biggest cuckoo. Google results for "World's Largest Cuckoo Clock," show both Sugarcreek, Ohio, which is home to the cuckoo clock pictured on the cover of the 1977 Guinness Book of World Records, and the one in Triberg. However, the one in the Black Forest claims to be larger than all others. I'll let you do the research, but I'm giving the Germans the win on this one.)

We wanted to keep dry and needed to kill some time until the magical hour of the cuckoo bird emerging from his hiding spot and thrilling spectators with his lyrical brilliance. The shop was crammed full of souvenirs—plenty to keep us entertained until the bewitching hour. After browsing for twenty minutes, we went back outside to join the throngs of people who were already gathering in the fog and rain for the magical moment. And so we stood in the rain, hoods up, glasses fogged up, and getting more wet and chilled by the minute.

At last ... only one more minute until the emergence of the mighty musical bird.

Tick ... tock ... the door began to open ... slowly.

At last, the bird emerged ... slowly ... ever so slowly ....

"Cuuuuuuuuuuuuuucccccccckkkkkkkoooooooooooooo."

"Cuuuuuuuuuuuuuucccccccckkkkkkkoooooooooooooo."

"Cuuuuuuuuuuuuuucccccccckkkkkkkoooooooooooooo."

"Cuuuuuuuuuuuuuucccccccckkkkkkkoooooooooooooo."

The bird sang? Chirped? Warbled? ... slowly ... four times, as it was 4 pm.

And then it retreated, and the door closed.

My glasses were fogged up and I could barely see. I looked at Richard and saw that his were fogged as well.

He turned to me and Sher, asking, "That's it?"

Sher and I looked at each other and burst out laughing.

"I guess that's it," I said.

"We drove all the way down here and stood out here, freezing in the rain, for THAT?" Richard asked. I laughed harder. And then he turned around and walked back to the car.

"Oh, oh, I think we're in trouble," I said to Sher, as she and I followed him, laughing so hard we could barely walk.

"But, hon, it's THE WORLD'S LARGEST CUCKOO CLOCK!" she called after him. "And now we can say we've seen it!"

He remained silent, got into the car, waited for us to get in and buckle up, and drove us out of town on our way to Munich.

I guess the Irish aren't as impressed with cuckoo clock culture as those of us of German heritage are.

***

And the rain continued.

We explored the main highlights of Munich, many of which I had been to already but was happy to visit again. And at the end of our first full day in Munich, we decided to try a Spanish restaurant that had excellent reviews on TripAdvisor. It was within walking distance of our hotel (where we had separate rooms this time!).

Richard plunked the name and address of the restaurant into the GPS, and we set out on foot. Now, keep in mind, this GPS was intended for use in a car. We figured that shouldn't matter; walking was obviously slower than driving, but we were still going from Point A to Point B, so the GPS should get us to our destination without any problems, just like it had done in Baden-Baden.

Ha.

Ha ha ha ha ha ha ha.

Wine, Bach, and Cuckoo Clocks

The GPS kept "recalculating" regardless of which street we went down and which direction Richard was facing. We knew we were within two or three blocks of the restaurant, but the technology was obviously confused. After wandering around in circles for ten minutes, we decided to look at the street signs and go in search of the restaurant as people had done for centuries before the invention of GPS. In the midst of the GPS/look-at-what's-around-us tug of war, we eventually found the restaurant and settled in for a Spanish meal.

We ordered our food—I was looking forward to a good pilaf and, of course, wine—and in doing so, got to chatting with our server, a delightful young woman who was obviously of Latino origin. She said that she was actually from Peru, not Spain, which piqued my interest.

"Which part of Peru?" I asked, assuming she would say Lima or some other major centre.

"Well, it's a very small town that many people haven't heard of, deep in the jungle. It's called La Merced."

"La Merced? Near Huancayo?" I asked.

"You know where Huancayo is?" she asked. "You've heard of La Merced?"

I'm not sure which of us was more shocked, as I told her why I knew of her town.

"When I was eighteen years old, I spent the summer living in Peru, working at a camp in the jungle a few miles outside of La Merced. And every Saturday, we would walk or hitchhike into La Merced to have lunch, do some shopping, and have ice cream!"

"Really!" she replied.

"Yes, and since I was there in 1988, I have looked for La Merced on maps, but I'd never been able to find the exact location. I only knew it was deep in the jungle, and it took us eight hours to get there from Lima, travelling by bus and then by cattle truck. I've always been curious to see on a map exactly where we were. I know it's near Huancayo, but also not terribly close. I've started to doubt that it exists, and I'm starting to think that summer was all just a figment of my imagination! But you're from there!"

"Yes!" she said. "It's my hometown!"

When I spent the summer of 1988 in Peru, I had no idea how big La Merced was; I knew it was a small-ish city in the middle of the jungle. More than twenty years after spending the summer in the jungle of Peru, I had travelled to Munich to finally find someone who could vouch for the fact that this town existed.

***

The next day, we embarked on the only fully guided day tour we took during our trip. We all wanted to see Neuschwanstein Castle, King Ludwig II's castle—the castle after which Disneyland's Sleeping Beauty's Castle was designed.

The rain and fog were relentless that day. The sky was overcast, and it seemed there would be no break from the rain all day. No matter—we were warm and dry on the bus and would remain there until we reached the castle.

Or so we thought …

We didn't realize that our itinerary included a stop at Marienbrücke (Queen Mary's Bridge)—a bridge that crosses over the deep Pöllat gorge and which was built by King Ludwig II so that people could enjoy a spectacular view of the castle. The king named the bridge after his mother, Queen Mary.

When the bus stopped and the tour guide gave us directions on how to get to the bridge, we set off in the rain. We had to walk several minutes to get to the bridge, and in spite of the rain, the place was teeming with tourists. Neuschwanstein is, after all, the most popular tourist attraction in Germany (even *more* popular than the WORLD'S LARGEST CUCKOO CLOCK), so there probably isn't any such thing as a quiet day to visit. Nevertheless, it is a sight to check off the list when one visits Germany, so we followed the crowds and politely waited at the entrance of the bridge until a gaggle of gawkers came off on our side, making way for us to step onto it and enjoy the view. The group on the bridge seemed to be taking their jolly sweet time, and I was starting to get impatient, wondering if we would be able to get on the bridge before we had to walk back to the bus.

At last, the group started to come our way and get off the bridge. As the last of them stepped off, we stepped on.

The tiny glimpse of the castle we had was breathtaking. The fog made it even more fairy-tale-like than it would have looked on a sunny day, I'm sure. A few steps in, we stopped and positioned our cameras just in time to snap a spectacular photo of … nothing. At the exact moment I brought my camera up to my face, the soup fog shifted, completely hiding the castle. I have a most impressive picture of trees on the left and right of the photo with a blob of white in the middle. When I show it to people, I assure them, "The castle is right there!"

We couldn't wait to see if the fog would lift because we had strict instructions on what time to be back on the bus. So after snapping my unique picture, I splish-splashed my way back to the bus, cursing the tourists who had taken so long getting off the bridge. Oh well. For a brief moment, I had *seen* the view, at least. And, after all, isn't that the point of visiting places in person—to see the sights with one's own eyes? If the picture was the goal, I could have stayed home and looked up pictures of the castle on the Internet.

The inside of the actual castle was opulent and certainly "fit for a king" with its ornate furniture, ceilings, wallpaper, and other decorations. King Ludwig II was apparently quite eccentric, self-indulgent, and extravagant; he spared no cost in building his hideaway in the Bavarian forest. We weren't allowed to take photos inside the castle. "As for the castle's placement at the top of a hill? Also completely unnecessary. He didn't need to see approaching armies; he simply enjoyed the view."[7] As did we. When we could see it.

***

I have now been to the concentration camp at Dachau three times. Once was enough, but when Sher and Richard and I were in Munich, they expressed interest in visiting for the same reason I wanted to visit when I went to Germany the first time; they wanted to see a concentration camp with their own eyes rather than rely for the rest of their lives on the images they have seen in media and in books. Then, when my sister and I travelled to Germany together a few years later, she also wanted to see it.

Sher and Richard told me that since I had already been there, they wouldn't be offended if I sat the trip out or did something else while they went, but I assured them I didn't mind going again, even though it wasn't a pleasant way to spend the afternoon.

They had a similar reaction as Mom and I had had. Silent contemplation on the way back to Munich.

As Richard drove us to Munich, I was sitting my spot—in the back seat, as if I were their kid—arranging my purse and other items that had piled up in the back when I discovered that the bag of the turkey potato chips was still there, and it still had a handful of chips in it. I picked it up and without opening it, stared at it for a few minutes, still wondering if it had been the chips that had made my stomach feel queasy.

"There's still some of these turkey chips left," I said. "Anybody want some?"

"No thanks, I'm fine," Sher replied.

"I'm good," Richard said.

I stared at the bag for a few moments. I didn't want to eat them. I was curious as to whether they had made me sick or not, but I was also too scared to open up the bag, take a whiff, and see how my stomach reacted.

"You know, after we had these chips the other day, my stomach wasn't feeling great," I admitted to them. "For a while I was thinking I might have to throw up, but thankfully it never got that bad."

"I felt the same way!" Sher said.

"Yeah, me too," Richard said.

Aha. Hypothesis confirmed.

When we got back to Munich, I pitched the bag of chips into a garbage can.

***

After a somber afternoon at the concentration camp, we needed to lighten our spirits. Before our trip, I had mentioned the Hofbräuhaus to Sher and Richard, and they decided it was on our to-do list. The evening after our outing at Dachau seemed like the perfect time for visiting this place as the food and music were sure to provide a good mental cleansing.

There's no bad time of day to go to the Hofbräuhaus, but it really gets rocking in the evening. It's a beer house, not a restaurant, so patrons walk in and find a seat somewhere. Anywhere. Seats can be

Wine, Bach, and Cuckoo Clocks

hard to find, and so visitors claim the first ones they see. And because many of the tables are large and long and seat eight to twelve people, patrons will likely find themselves sitting with strangers who could be from anywhere in the world. An oompah band plays all day and night, and the band members are all dressed in Lederhosen (the leather pants, short or long, with suspenders that are the traditional outfit for men in Bavaria). The servers are mostly women dressed in Dirndl (the traditional dress women in Bavaria wear; Dirndl have a full skirt and tight bodice), and the most amazing feat they perform is carrying up to six one-litre steins of beer in each hand.

We found three seats near the bandstand, ordered our food and beer, and sat back to enjoy the music, the atmosphere, and the beer while waiting for our meals. The band follows a routine. Every few songs, most of which are polkas, they pause, instruct the patrons to lift their glasses, and play "Ein Prosit," a short song for toasting to one another's health. Everyone sings along as loudly as possible, raises their glasses, clinks with those around them, takes a big swig, and then resumes the visiting and eating.

And perhaps dancing.

We had no idea where he came from, but all of a sudden, a short man, all smiles, with thick glasses, was exuberantly gesturing to Sher to dance with him. She laughed and politely refused, but he was having none of it. He wasn't obnoxious or physically aggressive, but his desire to dance with her was as persistent as his wide smile. Richard and I weren't helping her cause any; we both started clapping and cheering, egging him on, pressuring Sher to get up and dance with him. She finally relented, and the two of them swung around the aisles in a polka. When the song ended, he brought her back to us, thanked her for the dance, bowed, and left the three of us laughing.

Every day is Oktoberfest at the Hofbräuhaus. All day.

Mother Knows Best

Christine typically takes her vacation time in August, and when I was teaching high school, I had July and August off, so we have often aimed to get together in mid- to late-August each year. As a bonus, her birthday and mine are within a week of each other that time of year, so we include a joint birthday celebration.

By June 2010, my mom had finished a year of chemo treatments but not without a great deal of struggle. She had been diagnosed in March 2009, and the surgery she had six weeks after her diagnosis had given us hope that she could be one of the 5 percent of people who survive pancreatic cancer. The doctors had said after the surgery, "We got it all." However, she'd had to postpone several chemo treatments because her white blood cell count wasn't high enough. What was supposed to be six months of chemo took almost a year because of these delays.

I had booked my flights to Germany for August 2010 several months prior to my trip, and as June came and went, Mom was clearly and rapidly deteriorating. Ironically, as soon as her chemo treatments ended, she began expressing how the same type of pain that had led to her diagnosis was back and was getting worse much more quickly than it had before her surgery and chemo. Obviously the cancer was back—and with a vengeance.

My sleep problems surfaced again. I began waking up in the middle of the night having minor panic attacks. My brain was telling me I had to wake up *immediately* because if I didn't, I would die, so I was forcing myself awake. One night, though, I didn't wake up before dying in my dream, and I was freaking out about having just died. Mom, who had been dead for a while in this dream, calmly took me by the arm, led me around and through groups of people we knew who were going about their daily lives, and told me, "See, it's not so bad. Being dead is the same as being alive. They just can't see you." I've held on to the image in this dream as a source of comfort, knowing my mom, and others, are with me every day even though I can't see them.

I started to question whether I should be going to Germany. By this time, I knew that 50 percent of people diagnosed with pancreatic cancer die within six months of diagnosis. Many only live a few weeks past that revelation. It had been well over a year since my mom's diagnosis, but the rapid deterioration of her health indicated that her remaining time was likely very short. I didn't want to be in Germany for two weeks and miss my mother's last days. I didn't know what to do, but as I tend to do, I suffered in silence, not verbalizing my quandary to anyone.

As is typical with mothers, though, mine knew exactly what I was thinking without me saying a word.

"Don't even think about cancelling your trip to Germany," she told me in one of our phone conversations in late June.

"What do you mean?" I played dumb.

"I know you're thinking of cancelling your trip."

"Well, I don't know."

"I don't want you, or your sister, or your dad, sitting around waiting for me to die. You and Christine have been friends for years. And you've done well to see each other every year even though you live across the world from one another. She's a good friend to you, and you enjoy Germany and the time you spend with her. Don't put your life on hold just because I'm sick. You need to go and have your vacation with her."

The decision was made for me.

I didn't want to be on the other side of the world when my mom died. But I knew cancelling the trip would only frustrate her, and the last thing I wanted to do was add more stress or guilt to her already-difficult life. If I cancelled my trip, she would badger me about it, still mothering me even though I was well over forty years old.

The trip was on.

But then I felt even more guilty.

My parents were living on an acreage at the time, twenty minutes from the closest town, and because of my mom's failing health, they decided to sell the acreage and move into town. In July, I was able to go with them to view the house they purchased a few days later, but the move took place when I was in Germany in August. My parents had lots of help: several of my aunts and uncles, my sister and her other half, and friends. But I felt I should have been helping. Instead, I was in Leipzig, Germany, battling my thoughts.

More precisely, I was stretched out on Christine's couch, reading, snoozing, and fighting with myself. I was going to spend five days in Poland, but while in Leipzig, I didn't do much.

Why am I here? I should be at home helping my parents. They looked after me my whole life; now, they need me. I shouldn't have come.

And since I did come, I should be out touring around visiting sites that I haven't seen, getting out to places I haven't been. Instead I'm just lazing around, reading, spending down time.

I didn't verbalize my thoughts to Christine. Again, as I'm prone to do, I stuffed everything inside.

But mothers ... and good friends ... can read the person they are close to, and without us ever talking about it on that trip, Christine knew that reading, watching movies, going for walks, going out for breakfast, and relaxing in the evenings with a good bottle of wine and a book or movie with her and her hilarious Irish husband (Alan) was exactly what I needed.

On her previous visit to Canada the year prior, the best opportunity for Christine to visit with my mom was during one of Mom's chemo treatments. I took Christine to the hospital and the three of us chatted while Mom sat with her arm stretched out to receive the poison. Christine later told me, "No offense but it was quite comforting to sit with your mom during her chemo treatment. I know it sounds strange, but I enjoyed it."

"She enjoyed and appreciated your visit too," I said.

After a few days of arguing with myself in Leipzig, I convinced myself that sometimes "being" with loved ones is more important than "doing."

We did venture out to see a few sights I hadn't seen such as The Bose House (the home of Bach's next-door neighbour, Georg Heinrich Bose, which now houses the Bach Archive) and St. Thomas Church, the Lutheran church where Bach worked as music director until he died. (Martin Luther also preached at St. Thomas Church in 1539.) Knowing my love of music and the need for calm at this point in my life, I am certain Christine purposely chose these two places, in particular, to soften my heart and bring me some peace. Sitting in St.

Wine, Bach, and Cuckoo Clocks

Thomas Church, imagining Bach at work directing the boys' choir and playing the pipe organ certainly did that.

***

I don't listen to a lot of classical music, but I took a few music classes in university when I was thinking of declaring a music minor in my teaching degree, so I learned a bit more about classical composers throughout the centuries and their music. But I had one particular gaping hole. Bach.

Music was one of my favourite classes in elementary school until grade six. For some reason, the powers that be who were in charge of writing Alberta curriculum at that time thought that grade six students would love to learn the biographies of famous composers, so instead of playing instruments and learning how to read music and play, ten-year-olds would be thrilled to take notes on this fascinating historical information. Every day we arrived in music class to see the chalkboards filled with our teacher's handwritten notes on the life of the composer of the day.

We were required to sit quietly, copy the notes from the chalkboard into our notebooks, and then hand in our notebooks for our teacher to review. If there was time remaining after the last kid had handed in their notebook, we could then play some instruments.

After three weeks, I'd had enough of that nonsense. I loved music, and my music teacher was a skilled pianist who always got us doing lots of singing and playing in class. I didn't understand why music class in grade six had to become a read-and-take-notes dullfest. I got bored.

She doesn't read our notes anyway, I convinced myself.

On the day of my sin, the composer of the day was Johann Sebastian Bach.

I dutifully opened up my notebook, took up my pencil, and began to write. Yes, write, *not* copy notes from the chalkboard. I looked up at the board now and then to make it look like I was copying the notes, but I wrote. I wrote madly. It flowed out of me. A completely original and therefore entirely inaccurate story of Bach's "life." As I wrote, I became more and more relaxed and enjoyed music class for the first time in several weeks.

When my classmates started handing in their notebooks, I quickly wrapped up my story, slapped my notebook shut, walked to the front of the classroom, and added my notebook to the pile.

She doesn't read our notes anyway, I told myself.

The end.

Until next music class.

Our teacher always handed back our notebooks at the beginning of class so that we could use them to write that day's notes. She handed back everyone's notebooks ... except mine.

Uh oh.

"It seems that one of you decided to not follow instructions last class and instead of writing the notes from the board, wrote their own story," she announced as she gripped my notebook.

Uhhhhh ohhhhh ...

I stared at my notebook in her hand.

She did *not* sound happy.

"This is what Lorna wrote in her notebook." She opened my notebook and read aloud every word I had written.

I was mortified. And terrified, wondering what my punishment would be. I desperately wanted the floor to open up and swallow me. I kept looking at the floor in front of my feet. Nothing.

As she continued, I heard some of my classmates snickering and giggling quietly off and on during parts of my story. I was so embarrassed and felt so ashamed—yet part of me was a little proud that at least some of my peers thought this was funny.

She slowed down, succinctly and loudly enunciating every word as she reached the end of the story:

"And. He. Died. At. The. Age. Of. Eighty-four. While. Eating. A. Chicken. Salad. Sandwich."

She slapped my notebook shut.

Several of my classmates broke out into full-blown laughter.

I wanted to die.

But I couldn't help but smirk a little. I thought it was a brilliant and dramatic ending to a famous life.

***

Wine, Bach, and Cuckoo Clocks

I learned a great deal more about Bach in one day in Leipzig than I did in music class. In the real story of his life, Bach was appointed Thomaskantor (musical director) at St. Thomas on May 30, 1723, and conducted the St. Thomas choir for twenty-seven years until he died in 1750, apparently of a stroke (to my knowledge, there's no mention of a chicken salad sandwich in the historic record).

St. Thomas Church is Bach's final resting place.

***

Back home, in addition to the move, my mother also had a CT scan. I called her the day of the scan from Christine's apartment, and she caught me up on the goings-on at home.

"The move was fine. We didn't need you. We had lots of help. Everything is organized. We just have lots of boxes to unpack, but most of that is stuff we don't even need."

And she informed me that she would have the results of the CT scan the day before I flew back home.

"Ok, I'll call you the night before I leave. Talk to you then," I promised.

Catching my flight from Frankfurt to Calgary required that I take the first flight of the day from Leipzig to Frankfurt, which meant being at the Leipzig airport by 7 am, a route I've done several times, so the night before I was scheduled to return home, I packed up everything except what I would need for the morning. Christine picked up the phone and dialed my parents' number. She chatted with my mom for a few minutes and then handed me the phone, sending me into my bedroom so I could talk to my mom in private.

After the call ended ten minutes later, I emerged from the bedroom, phone in hand, and looked at Christine and Alan, who were looking expectantly at me.

I took a deep breath.

"The cancer is back. They found multiple spots on her liver, and she said there is a 'shadow' around her liver. It's spread throughout her internal organs, and they can't do surgery like they did last year."

Christine got up from her chair, walked into the kitchen, opened the fridge and a cupboard door, and came back to the dining room table, where she and Alan had been sitting. She placed a bottle of vodka and three shot glasses on the table, pulled out a chair, and sat down.

"We drink to your mother," she said, as she poured out three shots of vodka. The three of us downed far too much vodka that night. Again, exactly what I needed.

The next day, I boarded my flight in Leipzig, changed planes in Frankfurt, and landed back in Calgary to begin, together with my sister, supporting my parents and leaning on my friends and extended family members through the last four months of my mom's life.

The Tears of Millions

Visiting Dachau three times did not numb me to the significance of the events that took place within those buildings. Each time I left Dachau, I spent time on the trip back to Munich reflecting on how we humans treat each other and why. It's a huge question.

Despite having seen this concentration camp three times, I had always wanted to visit Auschwitz to see what this infamous place looked like. In the summer of 2010, when I visited Christine in Leipzig, I added a five-day stint to Poland. I took the train from Leipzig to Berlin and then flew to Kraków. Auschwitz is a day trip from Kraków, so I signed up for a guided bus trip for one of the days I was in Poland.

When I first arrived at Auschwitz, I was surprised at the serenity of the site. I think I expected my first glimpse of it to evoke similar feelings within me that Dachau had: solemn deliberation, reverence, a bit of dread. However, the brick buildings and the tall, thin trees lining the pathways could have easily been mistaken for a welcoming residential neighbourhood. It seems disrespectfully ironic that these stunning red brick buildings, which looked similar to the apartment complexes I saw in Dublin, housed the horrors that they did. I didn't know until my visit that prior to becoming a concentration camp, these buildings were used as a military base. All my life, I had only associated this place with the atrocities we learned about in high school.

Between the buildings stand towering trees, which had been planted shortly after the end of World War II. Now, after several decades, the trees have grown enough to stand tall and strong, as if they represent the ultimate triumph over the evils that happened there. The green of the trees in summertime provides a serene contrast to the blood-red brick of the former barracks.

Going through Auschwitz is only possible through a guided tour. As we went building to building, I bowed my head in places: in the room that was full of suitcases—luggage brought there by folks who had no idea they would never need the possessions they packed; in the room where an entire wall of hair is displayed behind glass; in the room containing an entire wall of empty gas (cyclone B) tins; and in the gas chamber. It was almost inconceivable to me that I was standing in front of the railroad tracks that had brought the prisoners to the site and the gate on which those famous words hang—the words that even those who don't speak a word of German may recognize: Arbeit Macht Frei.

The most sobering moment for me, though, was roughly two-thirds of the way through our tour when we were trapped inside one of the buildings because of a sudden downpour. Our guide paused our tour during the quick, sudden storm. I stood at a window, focused on the rain, and thought, *How ironic that I'm trapped inside this building. But I know I will get out. My having to wait is not remotely comparable to the anguish, confusion, and helplessness those people trapped inside these buildings all those decades ago must have felt.*

As I watched the raindrops smash against the glass, I thought, *These are the tears of millions of people. Not just those who died here, but of those who survived, knowing that their ancestors, their family members, their neighbours, their friends, were tortured and tormented within these buildings. These are the tears of millions of prisoners who died but also those who survived.*

The rain stopped as suddenly as it began, and our guide resumed our tour. As we left the building, I looked at the displays on the wall beside the door showing the pictures and names of a fraction of the people who had been taken there. I almost didn't want to look at the names; I dreaded seeing a last name that I would recognize, fearing that I may find a personal connection to this place. I scanned a few names and ventured out into the mud before I saw any that were familiar.

When our tour ended at the site's exit, I saw the shop was selling ice cream and people were buying ice cream cones and laughing while licking their double scoop. What a contrast to what was only a few feet away on the other side of the railroad tracks. Ice cream reminds me of birthday parties, having a treat on a sunny summer day. It's the food of fun and festivities.

I wasn't sure how to feel about the fact that they were selling ice cream there. Was it disrespectful? Or was it a symbol of hope and positivity? A symbol that there is good in the world, and that we have, at least in some ways, come a long way since those days of evil? After all, we can't linger in the past and we can't dwell on the negative, but the contrast between the wall of hair and the ice cream only steps away from each other left me feeling unsettled.

***

Before I left Leipzig for Kraków, Christine gave me one warning:

"Don't try to speak German there. The locals won't like it. Stick to English."

I didn't have any other options since I didn't know a single word of Polish other than perogy. Anytime I travel somewhere, I try to learn a few phrases so I can at least say hello and thank you in the local language, but I arrived in Poland not knowing even that much yet. I took note of her advice and reminded myself to speak only English in addition to any Polish phrases I could pick up.

At times when I was walking down the street, locals stopped me to ask me a question. I had no clue what they were asking, so I replied in English, "I can't speak Polish." Some of them seemed surprised. I guess I blended in.

One of my favourite classical composers is Chopin, and while he wasn't from Kraków, he *was* from a small town fifty-some kilometres from Warsaw, Poland, and when I saw there was a small, informal concert of Chopin music in a historic house, I decided to attend.

I was the first to arrive, half an hour early. The venue was small. The grand piano stood at the front of the room, and sixty or fewer chairs were set up.

As I waited, other attendees started to enter. None of them sat near me as there were plenty of spaces, but as the start time got closer and the room filled a bit more, a pleasant-looking, soft-spoken elderly gentlemen spoke to me. He was in his sixties or seventies.

"I don't speak Polish," I said to him.

He paused, remaining at my side.

After a few seconds of silence, he tried again.

"Sprechen Sie Deutsch?"

Ah. He was trying in German. Obviously he did not speak English.

Christine's warning rang in my ears, but this man had initiated the German, so I responded.

"Ja, aber nicht so gut. Ich verstehe nur ein bisschen."

"Ist hier frei?" he asked pointing at two seats in front of me.

"Ja, bitte." I gestured to the empty seats.

And so he and his wife sat down in front of me.

I could attend a symphony concert many days of the year in Calgary. But for the same reason I had a Singapore sling when I was in Singapore and a Peking Duck dinner when I was in Beijing, I wanted to attend this concert and listen to Chopin music in this room only three hundred kilometres south of where Chopin was born. Partaking of something in or near its origins makes it more meaningful for me. I sat, eyes closed for most of the hour-and-a-half concert, soaking in the études and nocturnes played by one man at a grand piano.

After the concert was over, the gentleman who had sat in front of me turned around, smiled at me, and wished me a good night. In German.

***

My family has a lot of their own dishes, many of which had German or Eastern Europe influence: pork with homemade sauerkraut, borscht, homemade noodles and other doughy dishes, and pickles. Lots of pickles. Mom used to pickle carrots and cucumbers, and her mom always had a lot of homemade pickled watermelon on hand. One of my dad's favourite appetizers when I was growing up was a dish of fresh, sliced onions soaked in vinegar.

And so when I started to see perogies on nearly every menu I picked up in Poland, I was thrilled. Blueberry, meat, sauerkraut, potato, cheese, potato and cheese. And chocolate. You name it, someone in Poland was putting it inside a perogy. I ate perogies every day and sometimes twice a day so that I could try as many options as possible. There wasn't a perogy that I put into my mouth that I didn't love.

On day three of my stay, while I was touring around, I was a bit hungry but not hungry enough to sit and have a whole meal. I wanted a snack. I popped into a small deli and examined their offerings in the display case and on the menu board. One of the menu items was pickles. Only pickles.

Perfect. I can just buy a pickle and that will tie me over until my evening meal. And this is Poland. The pickles are sure to be great!

I ordered the single menu item of "pickle" by pointing to the pickles, which were each the size of a small zucchini, and holding up one index finger.

It's huge, but that's OK. It'll be a great snack.

The young woman behind the counter took my money and a few moments later handed me a paper plate with a fork and three of the monstrous pickles.

I smirked as I ate one of them. There was no chance I could finish the other two, but I hated to waste, so I rolled up the paper plate and stuffed them into my bag.

***

The timing of my trip to Kraków was lucky. Oskar Schindler's factory building in the Podgórze district had opened as a museum six weeks prior to my arrival.

The factory is a bit tricky to get to. It's not in a main part of town where tourists would normally go, so it takes some seeking out. When I arrived, I noticed that some visitors were coming and going by taxi. I had taken a bus and then walked several blocks, checking Google Maps to make sure I was going the right direction.

It had the typical photo displays with explanations. Artifacts with explanations. Audio commentary. It was a well-organized and informative museum, one I was glad I had visited despite my general dislike for museums. It was, after all, humbling and inspiring to be standing in the building that had served to help so many who would otherwise have ended up in concentration camps.

What struck me most about the museum, though, was its tone. The tone was different from the World War II museums and other memorial sites I was used to seeing. Other than Auschwitz, the World War II historic sites I had seen were in Germany. I left Schindler's museum thinking, *Isn't it interesting that history may be based on facts, but it's so open to perspective.*

The sites I had been to in Germany were all tastefully presented. The Germans certainly do not shy away from the atrocities of World War II that their country was responsible for. But the information presented is all so factual, so unbiased, so impersonal. As I walked through and then away from Schindler's museum, I thought, *The Germans present World War II history as "This is what happened. This is what happened. And this is what happened."* This museum, however, presents the information as *"This is what those bastard Germans did to us."* I wondered if other World War II museums in Poland and other countries had the same underlying message.

Of course they didn't use those exact words, but there was no mincing words at Schindler's factory. The tone clearly laid blame on Germany for the actions they were, of course, responsible for. In the sites I have visited in Germany, the tone is neither apologetic nor blaming. It is factual and unbiased. "This happened."

My cousin Anke, who lives in Berlin and is about ten years younger than I am, told me she felt the same way when she visited Poland.

"I did this tour in the Warsaw Ghetto, and by the end of the tour, I didn't want to say I am German anymore because I felt so ashamed about what the Nazi Germans did, how brutal and cruel they were and sneaky but with cruelty. My shame wasn't a result of anything locals said or did, but it was the way the tour guides explained what happened. The local people were very nice to me, but it freaked me out to learn how cruel the Nazi Germans were and that they were telling their lies to manipulate the people. I have no real memories of how World War II was taught in school. In my memory, I found out about the Holocaust after I was twenty-two years old."

***

One site in Kraków made me cry in public and without shame.

In the district of Podgórze, parts of the Kraków Jewish ghetto still exist. In April 1941, using forced Jewish labour, a wall was constructed to separate the ghetto from the rest of the city. The wall was made of barbed wire and stones that were designed to look like tombstones. Today, some sections of the wall are still standing, and the stones are clearly visible.

As I walked along the sidewalk, the remaining sections of the wall at my side, I looked at the wall, softly running my hand along the tombstone-shaped stones. I wondered what the people living behind these walls must have felt, knowing that they had been rounded up and sent to live in this specific area simply because of their genetics.

I then turned and looked at Ghetto Heroes Square, called Zgoda Square prior to and during World War II.

The Jews who were moved from Kraków to Zgoda Square were only allowed to bring twenty-five kilograms of belongings with them. The rest of their possessions were confiscated.[8] The Jews were herded to the western part of the square. Trucks filled the centre of the square, and the goods stolen from the Jews were loaded onto these trucks. "A bloody selection [officials decided who would be killed and who would be sent to labour camps] took place on the square including the first selection in the Kraków ghetto on 4th June 1941, when at least 111 people were executed by firing squad."[9] The last selection took place on March 14th, 1943. Five years later, the Kraków City Council renamed the square Ghetto Heroes Square to commemorate the Jews who were murdered there.[10]

After selection, sorting of the confiscated belongings began. Items of value were moved to warehouses, and those deemed worthless were thrown into the streets. The unused, unwanted furniture dumped and piled in the square served as inspiration for the memorial that the square has become.

There are two types of chairs in the square. Oversized chairs in the middle of the square serve a symbolic purpose. All but two face the Eagle Pharmacy, which was a safe haven for Jews during World War II. It became a secret meeting place for Jews to meet and talk. The owner, Tadeusz Pankiewicz, also smuggled food, passed information, and provided free medicine for the Jews, and at times he hid people, enabling them to escape being sent to the death camps.[11] Of the two chairs not facing the pharmacy, one is set looking in the direction that the executions took place and the other faces Plaszów, one of the death camps the Jews were taken to.

The rest of the chairs are of standard size and serve a functional purpose. Visitors can sit and contemplate the meaning of the square.

As I looked at each of the identical chairs, I tried to envision the people who had been displaced in this area several decades earlier. Men, women, and children carrying suitcases, small pieces of furniture, clothing. Relocating against their will. Forced to leave their homes on a moment's notice, taking only what they could carry. Not knowing that even those meagre belongings would be taken from them.

How did they choose what to bring with them? What items did they leave behind but wish they could bring? How agonizing were those decisions? And what emotions ran through them as they were leaving their homes, suitcases in hand? Confusion? Fear? Hope? Uncertainty?

Individual chairs were mounted on small wooden platforms, each placed on the cement ground. The chairs lined up symmetrically to emulate the lines of Jewish people during roll call.

I sat on one of the chairs. It was appropriately cold. And hard.

I thought back to stories I had heard as I was growing up of people during World War II who thought they were being moved temporarily and would be soon going home and back to their normal lives, only to be sent to a concentration camp and forced into slave labour.

After sitting for several minutes, I stood again and took some pictures. The shadows. The lines. The lack of colour and the angular shape of the chairs against the simple, grey ground.

These single items of furniture, all identical, represent the hope that these people had in carrying their prized possessions through the square en-route to their new homes. Yet, they also represent the simplicity and bareness of these people's lives from that moment. How few material possessions they had. How all they had was hope. And how, at times, they even lost that.

I also envisioned my ancestors, moving across Europe centuries ago, carrying with them all they could take. Surely their possessions were meagre as, in those days, there was no help from DHL, FedEx, or UPS to ship prized possessions across a country or a continent or an ocean.

What belongings did my ancestors take with them through Poland on their way from Germany to Russia centuries years ago, in hope of a new, more prosperous life? And what did they bring on the ships that carried them across the Atlantic to this continent —another place of hope that they had only heard of?

Cruising the Baltic Sea

My sister, Janice, had been expressing to me for several years that she was interested in visiting Germany. Since I had established a routine of going there every two years so that Christine and I could maintain our yearly visits, I invited my sister to come with me on my next trip, a year and a half after our mom died.

That trip in August 2012 coincided with Christine, Alan, her parents, and Sarah (one of her nieces) going on a Baltic cruise, so would my sister and I like to join them? I was game and posed the option to my sister. We could do the cruise and then spend some time travelling around Germany. She hesitated because she had been on one cruise previously and hadn't found it to be her preferred way of travelling. The Baltic cruise stopped in Copenhagen, Stockholm, Tallin, and St. Petersburg. Janice thought it would be interesting to see these cities and agreed to go with me. Christine booked the cruise for us.

***

The two of us arrived in Germany the night before the cruise with only enough time to have a short visit with Christine and Alan before going to bed at their house.

The next morning, the four of us took the train to the northern coastal town of Kiel, Germany, where we met up with the rest of Christine's family members who were taking the cruise.

I've never felt the pull to travel by cruise ship. Yes, the convenience of visiting different countries without having to lug suitcases around is a huge plus, but I like to take chunks of time to explore cities and countries, often travelling with a loose agenda, which allows me to be spontaneous and explore. Still, I'm not one to say no to a new opportunity, especially one that falls under the "adventure" title. A Baltic cruise sounded like a great way to get a taste of each of these northern countries.

Wine, Bach, and Cuckoo Clocks

The bus pulled up, and we saw the word Schmetterling (butterfly) plastered on the side with a huge picture of a big blue and black butterfly beside the word. I'm not sure why but Schmetterling was the name of the bus company. It's not a word I use, but because of the way it rolls off the tongue, the word has stuck in my mind.

***

I had never been on a cruise before, but my sister had, and Christine's parents had been on several, so they knew that it would be easiest and most cost effective to pay for the all-inclusive drink package rather than paying for drinks one by one. Shortly after we all settled into our cabins, we went to the bar and paid for the drink package.

We then did some exploring, figuring out where to get our meals and drinks, where the lounge was so we could enjoy some drinks and live music in the evening, and where the pool was (on the top deck). We planned to spend our time on the ship enjoying the pool and taking in any other activities we could fit in.

The cruise line catered to their typical clientele: Germans, Italians, some English-speakers, and Russians, so when we played bingo—which Christine, Alan, Sarah, and I did anytime it was scheduled—we had plenty of time to find and mark our numbers since the numbers were called in all four languages. I already knew the numbers in German and quickly learned them in Italian, so by the time the English numbers were called (last), I had already marked my card. Unfortunately, none of us won anything.

Bingo was something fun we could do as a group, especially since Christine's niece was twelve and couldn't join us in the lounge at night.

From the first day, Christine, Alan, Janice, and I established a routine of spending an hour or two in the lounge each evening after dinner to enjoy a couple of drinks and listen to the live music. The lounge singer was cheesy; he turned every song into an 80s-style rock ballad. He was wearing a sparkly black blazer and took himself way too seriously, but we enjoyed the music and the atmosphere. Our evenings in the lounge were a welcome contrast to the busy days we had both at sea and on land.

Our first stop was Copenhagen. Unfortunately, none of the ship's tours for any of the ports were in English, and my German isn't good enough to fully understand much less translate for my sister what the tour guides would be saying. Nor did I want to put that kind of pressure on Christine; after all, it was her holiday, too. Knowing before we left Canada that the ship's tours were not in English, my sister did some groundwork and booked us on other tours for all stops except Copenhagen, which was the only stop she could not find tours in English for us. Left to either spend time touring ourselves around Copenhagen or join a tour that was in a language we didn't understand, we decided to join a German tour since, despite the language barrier, we would at least easily and efficiently be taken to the main attractions in the city.

We signed up for a half-day canal tour, which took us to the statue of The Little Mermaid and gave us a great glimpse of the local architecture. We didn't get much out of the narration during the tour, but we enjoyed cruising around on the water and seeing the highlights of the city. Whenever I could, I latched on to some key words and threw a bit of info at my sister, but for the most part, what we got out of the tour were the sights, not the sounds of a tour guide.

After the canal tour, we had a bit of extra time, so we wandered down some streets to do a bit of window shopping.

On the cruise, we were freezing our asses off, but Copenhagen was smoking hot that day. All we wanted to do was find a cold beer. We went into what looked like a small convenience store with a couple of tables for customers to sit at. We each bought an ice-cold Carlsberg and sucked them back good and fast. My sister isn't a beer drinker, but it was so hot that day and she said, "Hey, when in Copenhagen, drink the local stuff." She admitted that on such a hot day, the beer was refreshing. Along with our beer, we ended our afternoon with a snack of some herring on rye bread. My sister and I both love pickled herring, so this local treat was a great way to finish our stop in Copenhagen. We then went back to the cruise ship in time to relax a bit, get cleaned up, and get to the dining room for dinner.

Dinners on the cruise gave our group a chance to spend some time together. Wine was a given, as we all enjoyed wine. The servers were pleasant and efficient, and the food was good. The servings were large, so we always left the table completely satiated.

Breakfasts and lunches, however, were a fair bit more frenzied. For some reason, everyone on the ship seemed to be in a panic when it came to the buffet, and many of the other passengers were quite rude. It wasn't even a cultural difference; everyone of every cultural group was desperate to get their hands on the food. Literally. I was horrified to see people grabbing rolls out of the buffet with their hands when tongs were right in front of them. Christine was the first to comment, "You would think we were in the middle of a famine!" People were constantly cutting in front of each other in the line, pushing past others in order to get what they wanted as quickly as possible.

***

Our itinerary promised a half-day stop in Stockholm. Earlier that year, in May, around the time we were starting to organize our tours, I learned that ABBA The Museum had opened. I knew my sister would want to visit, and I certainly wanted to see the museum. I messaged Christine asking if anyone on their end would like to go with us. Absolutely. She, Alan, and Sarah wanted to see it, so I purchased tickets for all of us. Tickets had an entry time, and when I checked the itinerary of the cruise ship, I booked the tickets for roughly two hours after we were set to dock in Stockholm, thinking that would give us plenty of time to disembark and find our way to the museum.

What none of us knew was that cruise ships cannot dock right at shore in Stockholm. The ships have to dock in the middle of the harbour, and passengers need to be shuttled from the ship to the shore. Obviously, several thousand people cannot be shuttled all at once.

Ship staff told us to line up in the lounge and send one person from our group to receive a ticket. Each ticket had a letter on it, and each letter was assigned a time. We were then to gather again in the lounge at the time corresponding to the letter on our ticket.

Christine and I stood in line to obtain the ticket for our group. As we were lined up, a group of tall young German men cut immediately in front of us in line. Christine said something to them—I didn't understand what she said. I could guess, though, and I could especially guess what they said to her in return by the look on her face when she glanced at me and started swearing in English telling me how rude they were being and how they were "an embarrassment" for her as a German. There was no getting our spot back from them, so we politely stood in line, taking comfort in thinking that karma would get them someday.

The letter we got was J.

Using my fingers to count, I realized that J put us likely in position for the tenth shuttle trip heading ashore.

They've done this a million times. They know what they're doing. It'll only be a few minutes before we get on the shuttle. We won't be waiting long.

The five of us—me, Janice, Christine, Alan, and Sarah—settled into some chairs to wait for our letter to be called.

A.

And we waited.

B.

And we waited.

And waited.

C.

Ten minutes lapsed between letters being called. At that rate, we weren't going ashore anytime soon.

We waited.

And waited.

A freakin' hour and forty minutes later, J was finally called. By this time I had looked at our tickets to the museum probably twenty times, wondering if we were going to make it to the museum at all. Our entry time was 11 am. Our ticket was finally called at 10:40.

We leapt up and made our way to the exit.

When we got ashore, we looked around for a taxi and found one right away.

We had no idea where this museum was. It could have been a forty-five-minute taxi ride for all I knew, but when we were in the taxi, I got onto my cell phone's data plan and googled it. It seemed to be a short drive around to the other side of the harbour.

Our taxi driver got us there in ten minutes. We paid him, rushed out of the vehicle, and ran up to the entrance of the museum, punching our tickets one minute before our entry time.

The museum is a great display of ABBA's history, their costumes, gold records, and other memorabilia. There are also interactive displays. This was my kind of museum. My sister's favourite section was the Polar Studio, a "recording booth" where we sang along to "Dancing Queen." We perused the gift shop and bought a few items. Neither of us have yet written in the journals we bought. We are saving them. For what, we're not sure, but they are nice, hardcover, black journals with "ABBA The Museum" etched on the front. We also both got a few giggles during our final moment at the museum—commemorating the occasion by stepping behind the board with faces cut out for a fabulous photo op. She and I were the girls, Agnetha (Janice) and Anni-Frid (me because I'm a wannabe redhead and had red highlights in my natural hair colour). Benny and Bjorn got to remain as themselves for the photo.

Our tour through the museum ate up all the time we had in Sweden. So there; I can say I've been to Sweden. Most importantly, I've been to ABBA The Museum. I'm not sure if anything else in Sweden would be as appealing to me as that museum is—one of the rare museums I've been to that I quite liked; I didn't have the chance to find out. And maybe I never will.

***

Next up was Estonia, which I had never heard of before we planned this trip. I assumed it was one of the countries that had been part of the former USSR.

Janice and I had mulled over the idea of touring ourselves around and looked at what there was to see and do in Tallin. There was a market. And the Museum of Occupations. Hmm. A museum about occupations. How interesting would a museum about different jobs be? It sounded odd and vehemently boring. I kept looking.

I came up dry, except the Museum of Occupations kept coming up in my Internet searches. It seemed to be the prominent tourist attraction in Tallin.

Occupations? Why would anyone go to a museum about different types of jobs, unless they were a high school student researching possible career paths? And why does Estonia, of all places, have a museum of occupations, of all things?

Erm, upon further investigation I discovered that the theme of the Museum of Occupations is the history of countries occupying other countries ... which makes sense in Estonia as it is a sovereign country, but it's got a lot of Finnish influence, and of course Russian. When you think of *that* definition of occupations, it makes sense to have a museum dedicated to it in nearly any Eastern European country. After all, every inch of Europe has been claimed by multiple rulers and countries over the centuries.

But then Janice found *the* tour—the one with our names all over it. A food and booze tour. We figured we needed to check out this part of Estonian culture.

When our ship docked, we disembarked at 7 am. For weeks leading up to our trip, we had been laughing about the fact that beginning at the crack of dawn, we would be spending the morning drinking in a country we'd never heard of before.

We made our way to the meeting point in the old part of the city and we waited. And waited. And waited. Yuri, our guide, was nowhere to be seen. After fifteen minutes, Janice tried calling the number she had. No answer.

Immediately after she disconnected the call, her phone rang, and it was Yuri calling her. He was late, very apologetic, and would be there in five minutes.

After five minutes, a young, blond man arrived, looking nonplussed as if he were on time rather than being half an hour late. No matter. The tour consisted of only me and my sister and we had lots of time; we set out on foot.

Yuri led us to a handful of places offering various types of alcohol, and at the final stop, we got to sample some local bread and cheeses. Some of the alcohols were unique—something I knew we would not be able to get in Canada, so Janice and I both spent a little money buying a licorice-flavoured liqueur and a cream liqueur with an egg yolk base. We also each bought an almost-neon red liqueur that was sickeningly sweet. I thought it would be good with club soda, and when mixed with soda, would also be a very pretty colour.

Wine, Bach, and Cuckoo Clocks

After the tour, we had a bit of time to spare so we went to the outdoor market, where I bought a heavy knit sweater in a cool-looking pattern that I thought was probably Estonian. It was, after all, August on the Baltic, and a heavy sweater seemed a logical addition to my suitcase. We had to relinquish our alcohol to the staff on the ship as we boarded, but they gave it back to us when the cruise was over.

The Baltic Plague

On the first day of the cruise, I had noticed a couple of people coughing and their coughs sounded nasty. I am prone to getting sinus infections, and I've had both pneumonia and bronchitis a few times, so I try to keep my distance from people who seem sick.

On the second day of the cruise, a few more people were coughing.

On the third day, still more were coughing.

Some affliction was making its way through the ship. The way I see it, a cruise ship is like a school classroom. Groups of the same people in close quarters, interacting with one another day after day. Whatever bug was going around the ship was spreading like soft butter on hot toast.

And so I got sick. *Really* sick, as I do any time I get a sinus infection. A deep, dry, chesty cough, sinus pain and congestion, fever, and aches. I went to the ship's pharmacy and got some cough syrup, which helped somewhat, but I was feeling awful.

No one else in our group was sick, but a significant and increasing number of people on the ship were.

Although I was the one afflicted with The Baltic Plague, Janice also suffered as a result of my illness. I've had sleep issues for as long as I can remember. According to my mom, I used to walk in my sleep as a child. She told me numerous times over the years how she sometimes found me outside wandering around the farmyard in the middle of the night. Apparently, my mom also discovered me wandering around the house at times: in the kitchen, living room, basement, and elsewhere. She would hear a noise, get up, and find me creeping around. I have no memory of these sleepwalking incidents or many of my nighttime traumas since then, including the one on the Baltic cruise.

My sleep issues are anxiety related, so anytime I have physical or mental distress, my sleep is impacted. Whenever I am sharing a room with someone, they also get to share the room with the demons that come out of me at night.

Apparently, a few days into my affliction with The Baltic Plague, I suddenly started screaming blue bloody murder in the middle of the night one night with no warning whatsoever, scaring the living shit out of my sister. I have no memory of this.

When she told me this the next morning, of course I felt bad for terrorizing her in her sleep, but what could I do?

Her update reminded me of the time she and I had been on a vacation to San Francisco together and something similar happened. One morning halfway through our trip, as we were getting ready in our hotel room, she asked me what had happened during the night.

"What were you trying to tell me last night?" she asked.

"What do you mean?" I asked.

"You started talking to me in the middle of the night, but I couldn't understand what you were saying."

"I don't remember trying to talk to you."

"You were. You said something that woke me up, so I asked you to repeat what you said. You replied, but it was complete gibberish. I had no idea what you were trying to say, so I kept asking you what you were talking about. You kept replying, but nothing you said made any sense. It was a complete two-sided conversation, but nothing you said was comprehensible."

"I have no memory of this whatsoever." I laughed as I continued getting dressed.

I think, by now, my sister thinks I am possessed by demons. Perhaps I am.

A similar incident occurred when I visited Christine in Dublin, Ireland, where she was working for three years in the early 2000s. I visited during spring break one year when I was still teaching and of course, she toured me around, taking me on day trips from Dublin. One such trip was to the Hill of Tara in County Meath, forty-four kilometres north of Dublin. The hilly, green area is an ancient ceremonial and burial site used by the Druids for animal sacrifices. Here, visitors can view the remains of twenty ancient monuments. The oldest tomb, Dumha na nGiall (the Mound of the Hostages), was built around 3,200 BC and holds the remains of hundreds of people.

The night after our visit to the bloody druid killing sites, I had a rough sleep. I was sleeping on an air mattress on the floor in Christine's living room and awoke in the middle of the night to find her kneeled at my side, patting and rubbing my arm. I sat up, surprised, and was scared to see her. She, too, was terrified. She had awoken to the sounds of what she said "sounded like an animal being tortured" only to find it was me.

She gently woke me up to rescue me from whatever dream I was having, which again, I had no recollection of. I must have been attending the sacrifices in my sleep.

***

By the time the cruise ship was headed for our last stop, St. Petersburg, I was plastered to my bed with The Baltic Plague. I was so sick that it took everything within me to get up and go for meals. The night before our stop in St. Petersburg, I was seriously considering cancelling. I couldn't see myself having the energy and stamina to survive a ten-hour tour throughout an entire city.

The next morning, I woke up feeling horrible. Utterly lousy. I wanted someone to blast a high-pressure hose through my sinuses to release the unrelenting pressure and congestion. Any relief would have been welcome. The medication from the ship pharmacy had proved to be almost useless.

However, I mustered up every ounce of strength I could and convinced myself to get vertical.

It's one day. I may never have the chance to visit any part of Russia again. I can do this. And the next two days are at sea, so I can stay in bed for two whole days straight after today and rest. Let's do this.

I heaved my pressurized skull and everything below it out of bed, showered, got dressed, and organized my belongings for the day trip.

What would have been wonderful was if the Higher Powers had taken pity on me and blessed us with a warm, sunshiny day to counter the misery I was feeling. At least some sunshine would have perked me up and felt nice on my sickly face.

Nope.

Wine, Bach, and Cuckoo Clocks

The weather that day was the worst of our entire cruise. All day, we were pushing back against gale force winds and torrential rains. Walking took a lot of strength because the winds were so strong. A few seconds after getting off the ship, my umbrella and my sister's flipped inside out, and thus they stayed for the rest of the day.

Our tour was a power-trip through St. Petersburg.

What is there to see in St. Petersburg? Palaces with gold and artwork everywhere, a fancy church, another palace with gold and artwork, an opulent subway station with gold everywhere, another palace with gold and artwork everywhere, a museum or two, another palace with gold and artwork everywhere ... the city has a truckload of stuff to see. Ten hours is probably enough to do two of the places (or is that *palaces?*) justice. We did E. V. E. R. Y. T. H. I. N. G. In ten hours. In torrential rain. With my sinuses feeling like they were being pinched by the world's strongest lobster. #Superawesomegoodtimes.

Oh, and because anytime we were outside, the rain was smashing down upon us, throughout the entire day, we looked like we had just emerged from a swimming pool. We took one photo: the two of us looking like drowned rats, holding our inside-out umbrellas, in front of some building that was plastered with gold. And cheesy smiles.

So about those palaces and stuff ... yeah, lots of gold. And statues. And fountains. And gold.

Peter the Great commissioned the building of Peterhof Palace, which is actually a series of palaces. In addition to the palaces, which are now museums with seemingly-endless rooms opulently decorated with fine furniture, artwork, and ornate wall and lighting fixtures, the property has numerous spectacular fountains throughout the gardens, dripping with gold statues. "There is plenty at Peterhof to keep you occupied for a whole day."[12] Our tour guide gave us an hour.

The Winter Palace was the official residence of the Russian Emperor from 1732 to 1917 and now houses the Hermitage Museum. The Hermitage is supposedly St. Petersburg's most famous visitor attraction, and while it's not as opulent as Peterhof, it contains reams of fine art and antiquities. The sheer size of the property and the art collection mean you could spend a lot of time there. "Optimal: One day for the Winter Palace and General Staff Building collections. Minimum: Two hours."[13] Here too, we had an hour.

The Church of Our Saviour on Spilled Blood is a uniquely colourful Russian Orthodox church. It was built on the site of the March 1881 assassination of Emperor Alexander II. "If you're on a whistlestop tour, there's no need to set aside time for the Church on [sic] Spilled Blood, as you're bound to pass it more than once in even the shortest exploration of St. Petersburg."[14]

We were on a whistlestop tour to beat all whistlestop tours but oh, we stopped! Yessiree, we stopped. Our guide warned us that pickpocketing is common in this church, so we were to closely guard our wallets and purses and even our cameras while we were using them. I held everything to my chest as we were herded through the church. It was so crowded it was almost impossible to move my arms to position my camera for a picture, and being paranoid of pickpockets, I didn't bother snapping any shots, but I did appreciate that we stopped at the church.

Palace palace palace, blah blah blah. I lived in Japan for three years, and after touring around, visiting different temples and shrines, over the course of those three years, we expats started to joke, as many people who travel Europe, Asia, etc. do, that they all start to look the same after a while. "You've seen one Buddhist temple/Shinto shrine, you've seen them all." Janice has also said she felt this way after extensive travels in Europe, visiting cathedral after cathedral. This sentiment is certainly not true, though, as there are multiple unique temples and shrines not only throughout Japan but in other Asian countries, too, and of course multiple cathedrals in Europe are also unique and spectacular.

My point is, when soaking up all of this culture, architecture, and history, there comes a point when your brain is saturated and the majesty of it all just bounces off of you. After blasting through these three gargantuan and luxurious sites in St. Petersburg, my brain was getting full.

Last on our list of palaces was Pushkin, also known as Tsarskoye Selo, yet another extravagant sight in St. Petersburg. Pushkin has two palaces portraying the wealth of the Romanov family. "Like Peterhof, Tsarskoye Selo is best enjoyed at a leisurely pace over a full day, with a break for a picnic in the park or lunch at one of Pushkin's restaurants. Minimum: There's no point in visiting Tsarskoye Selo unless you have a full morning or afternoon free."[15] Guess how much time our guide gave us here? I'll give you a hint: not a full day. Nor a full morning or a full afternoon. You know. Our pace as we toured Puskin, as it was at all the other palaces, was not leisurely.

Before our ship had docked in St. Petersburg, I knew we were going to be spending the day touring fancy schmancy Russian palaces; I knew St. Petersburg was deeply connected to the royal history of Russia. What I didn't know is that St. Petersburg also has a spectacular subway station—one that is functional but also serves as a tourist attraction. Admiralteyskaya, at 105 metres underground, is the deepest subway station in Russia. From the top of the escalator, it's not possible to see the bottom. At the bottom of the long escalator ride are spectacular mosaics and other pieces of art on the walls.

The station contains several mosaics, in gilded frames, showing the maritime history of Russia. One of the most spectacular is a small mosaic painting above the archway from the first escalator depicting Neptune, the god of the seas, on his chariot.

***

I saw more gold that day than I'm sure I likely will in the rest of my life put together. St. Petersburg is worth visiting. But maybe, just maybe, take more than a day to do so. And go when the sun is shining unless you want to look like a sea troll at the end of the day and you enjoy battling torrential Baltic storms.

But ... I've been to Russia. And I have the stamps in my passport to prove it.

However, we had one not-so-minor glitch at the end of our long day tour.

We had left our ship with strict instructions, as we had on the other stops, to be back at a certain time as the ship was scheduled to leave and there would be no waiting for tardy passengers. We were to be on the ship at 6:30 pm sharp. They would close the door at 6:30 and if we weren't on board, we would get left behind.

Our tour was scheduled to end at 5 pm, so we had not been concerned throughout the day until later in the afternoon when our bus was headed back to where all of the cruise ships were docked. Our tour was running forty-five minutes late. The traffic was heavy and slow-moving, and we had no idea how far away we were from the dock. Janice asked our tour guide how far away we were and reminded her that we had to be back on the ship by 6:30. Our guide assured us that we would be back in time despite the slow, rush-hour traffic.

As 6 pm rolled around, we saw the cruise ships ahead of us and felt a bit of relief.

We were going to make it in plenty of time.

But then we stopped at the first ship to let off some of the other members of our tour group. And then the next ship. The tour guide told us our ship was the last one on the dock and so we would be dropped off last. Other members of our tour group started to chime in, telling our guide that their ships weren't leaving until later and that we should be dropped off first. For some reason, the driver and tour guide stuck to their plan, dropping everyone else off first. By 6:20, we were still dropping other passengers off and there were still several other ships before ours.

There was one other detail: We had to go through border control and have our passports checked and stamped by customs officials before we could get back on our ship. We were still far enough away that we couldn't see the checkpoint in front of our ship. We had no idea how long the line would be to go through customs.

We started to panic.

I had visions of getting left behind in frickin' Russia of all places. Not Sweden, not Denmark, not even Estonia. Frickin' Russia. The place my ancestors had fled from. And the one place that our cruise docked where we had to get a visa. Ours was a one-day tourist visa, and here we were, on the verge of getting trapped in the country, watching our cruise ship sail away. I was terrified that if we overstayed our visa we'd end up in some Russian prison.

Plus, we'd be in Russia while all of our belongings were on the cruise ship, except our purses and an inside-out umbrella, and the cruise ship was at sea the next two days. We'd have no chance to get back on the ship before the cruise ended. We'd have to find a way back to Germany if we managed to escape the Russian authorities.

At the last stop before ours, we finally glimpsed the customs booth we would be going through and saw that there was no lineup. It was 6:25, and we would surely make it. But then, the last people in our group stuck around talking to our tour guide outside of the bus for a couple of minutes. There seemed to be an issue with them wanting to tip her but not having the right amount of cash, and there was some commotion trying to resolve this issue. My sister and I had had it; we stuck our heads out of the bus and hollered.

"We need to go! It's almost 6:30!"

At that, the tour guide extracted herself from the last members of our group, got back on the bus, and directed the driver to take us toward our ship.

When the driver stopped, I thrust some money into our tour guide's hand and thanked her over my shoulder. Janice and I bolted to the customs booth.

Fortunately, there was no one in line and the Russian customs officer was not feeling overly chatty. He stamped our passports without a word, and we then sprinted to our ship, boarding at 6:29.

Our dinner reservation was also set for 6:30, so we rushed to our cabin, dropped off our bags, and then ran to the restaurant to join Christine and her family for dinner.

"Janey Mac!" Christine exclaimed as we rushed up to the table. "What happened to you two?"

We flopped down in our chairs and tried to catch our breath.

"We almost got left behind!" I huffed.

There we sat, hair pasted on our heads, shirts and pants that had been soaked and dried and soaked and dried throughout the day. We were gasping for air since we had just sprinted from the bus drop off to the ship and then all the way through the ship so as to make it in time for dinner. And I'm sure we were stinky.

Around the table sat Christine, Alan, Christine's parents, and Sarah, all clean and relaxed. They had come back from their tour, showered, changed clothes, did their hair. Makeup. Jewelry. Dresses and dress shirts and pants. Nice shoes. And there we were, the two hicks from Canada who almost got stranded in Russia, looking like we had been rescued at sea from a lifeboat that had been drifting for days.

Thankfully, the server came immediately to take our wine order.

***

The only reason I had gotten out of bed the morning we went to St. Petersburg was the thought that this was quite possibly my only chance to set foot in Russia in my lifetime, and after soldiering on through the day, I would have two days at sea to do nothing but rest, sleep, and try to recover. Had we not had those two days at sea, I may have opted out of the St. Petersburg tour, but I told myself I could find a chair by the pool, get some sunshine, enjoy the fresh air and summer heat, and relax and recover.

For the next two days, I plopped myself onto a deck chair by the pool, read my book, and rested. In the Baltic air. Baltic. North.

Have you ever been on the Baltic Sea? It ain't the Mediterranean.

According to The Online Slang Dictionary, the definition of the word Baltic is ... "cold."[16] That's it.

Those two days at sea were sunny but there was no nice warm sea breeze to accompany the sun like there is in the Caribbean. There was a chilly wind.

We all spent those two days by the pool, but for the love of God not *in* the pool—it was *never* warm enough for that—reading, visiting, snoozing, while wearing sweaters and wrapped in blankets. My Estonian sweater that I bought to wear at home in the winter turned out to be a useful purchase.

But I did start to feel better over those frigid days.

By the time the cruise ended. I was on the mend, but The Baltic Plague had moved on to Janice. Our first stop on dry land after the cruise was a doctor's office, where she was taken in to see a doctor immediately upon checking in. She told me that the doctor was pleasant and impressed her; she was prescribed antibiotics, which took a few days to kick in, but once they did, she too was on the mend.

Overall, I enjoyed the cruise other than getting sick and having to wait so long to get to shore in Stockholm. The former could have happened on any trip (and it certainly has. I've gotten bad sinus infections a few times while travelling.) But those were minor annoyances.

I'd been genuinely terrified at the possibility of getting stranded and apprehended in Russia. As our bus was still inching toward our cruise ship, I started to plan our next few days. If we didn't get arrested, we'd have to find a hotel room in St. Petersburg and then find a flight

Wine, Bach, and Cuckoo Clocks

back to Germany and meet our cruise ship in Kiel, as St. Petersburg was the final stop before the last few days at sea. I wasn't sure how we'd get back to Germany, and of course there was also the issue of our visas being one-day tourist visas because we were on a cruise ship. If we had overstayed our visa, who knows what kind of legal implications would have been in store for us. I tried to reassure myself thinking, *Well, we have our credit cards. Hopefully this is the kind of situation that, as long as we have access to money, we can get our asses out of Russia.* But I was well aware that with our expired visas, Russian authorities could have made our lives very difficult. I was relieved that I didn't have to find out what would have happened.

Other than that, I tried to roll with everything during the cruise, as I do when I travel, and not stress about the events that I can't control. The last time I went to Japan to visit former colleagues and students, I arrived at the airport the day after the Fukushima nuclear power plant had blown up. Bring on the disasters. It's all good; I'll figure it out. Just don't leave me behind in Russia.

Wine Time

Janice trusted me with many of the details of our trip, but she also did a fair bit of research into Germany and in the process, compiled a list of cities she wanted to visit. She also checked out a few options for accommodation.

Berlin was a must stop, as it's a city of great history and culture. Since the Wall came down years ago, Berlin is no longer divided, and it's possible to move throughout the city without even noticing where the boundary used to be. Small sections of the Wall are still standing; they remain, covered in graffiti, as reminders of the political division that once was. I had never seen the sections that are still standing, so we headed there first, took our token photos, and resumed wandering around the area.

The area of Berlin near Checkpoint Charlie, the best-known crossing point between the former East and West Germany, is busy and touristy. Panelled displays describe the history of the Wall, and the streets are full of souvenir shops, sections of the Wall that remain, and markers on the pavement indicating where the Wall used to be. I'm sure I'm one of millions who have taken a photo of myself with one leg on each side of the marking on the street—one foot in each country.

Another attraction in this area is the booth indicating the actual checkpoint. "Soldiers" in full military garb will pose with visitors for pictures, and there is a steady lineup of tourists waiting for this opportunity. We did not. As we were walking away, Janice said what I had always felt but never vocalized in the several times I had previously visited the area:

"It kinda bothers me that they're doing that."

"You mean posing for pictures in the uniforms?" I asked.

"Yeah, I think it's disrespectful to what people in East Germany went through when the Wall was up. It comes across to me as making fun of the whole situation. But then what do I know?"

Wine, Bach, and Cuckoo Clocks

I nodded, remembering that I had heard families had been separated when the Wall went up. I thought of Christine growing up in the former East Germany. Over the years, she has told me stories about what she and her family experienced behind the Wall. Those stories are not mine to tell, but I will say that those of us who were born and raised in a free, democratic society cannot begin to empathize with people being forced to spy on family members, being *told* what career they would pursue, and seeing family members taken away for a few days only to return and never speak of what they experienced during their disappearance. I've been in and near World War II and Cold War museums and monuments with Christine, and the look on her face and her body language in those moments indicate to me what direction our conversation should take. I don't push, and I don't ask. If she opens the conversation, I take part and tread cautiously, eager to listen and learn, but if she doesn't, we discuss other topics.

Janice and I didn't go into the souvenir shops in the streets surrounding Checkpoint Charlie. We left that area quickly as we were both bothered by the way tourists and the "soldiers" were posing for pictures: making the peace sign, smiling, posing as one would if they were at Disneyland taking a selfie with Mickey and Minnie. We made our way to the Brandenburg Gate, snapped our token photos there, and explored other areas of Berlin.

Berlin is known for its punk scene and artsy vibe. It's a quirky place with numerous dance clubs, edgy music, and unique landmarks. As a result of Janice's research before our trip, she suggested one place for us to stay while in the city. She's a fan of Anthony Bourdain and had seen him, on his TV show *Parts Unknown*, talk about a unique hotel in Berlin that she thought would be fun to try. She was under the impression he had stayed there but after we got home from Germany she learned that he hadn't stayed there; he'd only done an episode profiling it.

At the time of writing this, the Propeller Island City Lodge's website says they are "closed for repairs and a new concept,"[17] and I'm curious as to what the "new concept" will entail. The concept when we stayed there was bizarre and fun, each room with its own theme, including unique shapes and furnishings. These are some of them:

- Flying Bed Room: the floor was tilted, and the bed was suspended above the floor.
- Four Beams Room: the bed in this room was also suspended; it was tied to four large ceiling rafters 1.6 metres above the ground, attached by thick ship rope. The website said, "Unfortunately, security regulations bar this from being rented out to overweight guests!"[18]
- Mirror Room: the walls and ceiling were entirely mirrored in this diamond-shaped room.
- Freedom Room: this room was designed to mimic a jail cell. The bed was a granite slab chained to the wall and included a thin mattress. There was a hole in the wall to give the sense that one can escape from the room, and the "cell" contained a toilet (the whole lodge had shared bathrooms).
- Padded Cell Room: the entire room was upholstered in green, padded leather.
- Coffin Room: Yes, this room contained two coffins for beds. Guests could sleep with the coffin lids open or closed. This room had signs plastered all over it: "Please do not have sex in the coffins; they will break."

I stayed in the Freedom Room and had a great sleep considering I was "incarcerated." My sister chose the coffin room.

When we met for breakfast the next morning, she looked a bit bedraggled. I asked her how she slept and suggested that perhaps the coffin room hadn't been a good choice? She said no, her bed wasn't the problem.

"It was the couple in the room next to me having wild, raging sex all night."

I had faintly heard the woman screaming because their room was down the hall from mine—but it was next to Janice's, and she wasn't impressed at their enthusiasm for whatever room they were in and whatever they were doing in it.

Wine, Bach, and Cuckoo Clocks

We had only booked one night at the Propellor, opting for a normal hotel for the rest of our stay in Berlin in case the Propeller was more about novelty than comfort.

***

Our trip to Germany was during a time when my sister had decided to take some sommelier courses to learn more about wine and pairing wine with food. She wasn't planning on being a sommelier, but she did want to up her knowledge of wines. She had been to a food and wine festival in Edmonton, where she was living at the time, a few months before our trip and had gotten the scoop on a couple of winemakers in the Rhein Valley, which has a plethora of said entrepreneurs and larger businesses. She wanted to visit two wineries in particular.

My sister knows good wine, so I let her lead the charge on this portion of our trip. We took our rental car and headed to the wine country along the Rhein.

Our first stop was the Rhein Hotel, owned by the Stüber family, where I had stayed a few years previously with Sher and Richard in the "two bed room." I knew my sister would appreciate the fine dining and enjoy the chance to stay at a homey hotel owned by probable relatives. There isn't much to do in Bacharach, so we had a wonderful dinner, walked around the town a bit, spent the night in the comfort of the cozy hotel owned by … our extended family? … and left the next morning for other parts of the wine area. I was thrilled to see that Andreas Stüber was keeping with his tradition of visiting every table to talk to his guests while they ate dinner. I re-introduced myself and told him there were two Stubers sitting at our table. He was pleasant and hospitable, as he had been on my previous visit, and the food was just as great. I thoroughly enjoyed my boar.

Our next stop was Trier, the biggest city in the Mosel Valley, near the French border. We made Trier our base as it had the best hotel options and was within short driving distance of the wineries my sister wanted to visit.

Her first winery choice was Dr. Loosen, a family winery that has been producing wine in the Mosel Valley for over 200 years. They are located in Bernkastel, less than an hour's drive from Trier. My sister had contacted the winery prior to our arrival and arranged for a tasting.

After we easily found a spot to park, we entered and Janice introduced herself.

I had never heard of this winemaker; there are countless wineries and winemakers in Germany. The German wines we get here in Canada are a fraction of what's available in Germany, and so many of the wines in Germany are great. Therefore, when I go to Germany, I expect to drink good wine made by winemakers that I've never heard of. Some of Dr. Loosen's wines are easy to find in liquor stores in Alberta, but as is the case with any winery, those on the shelves in Alberta are only a small sample of what the winery produces.

We sampled some of their wines, and then my sister began the business negotiations. She wanted to take a case of wine home.

I'd been to Germany enough times to know that Germany is overflowing with great wine. I could easily spend hundreds of dollars on good wine that we can't get back home, but I limit myself to bringing home a bottle or two since we also have no lack of good wine available in Canada. To me, it's just not worth the hassle of trying to bring more than two bottles, and enjoying the wines when I go to Germany is one of the many reasons I look forward to going there.

But she was on a mission.

Her ten bottles selected (I chose two), she paid for them and gave the staff member her address so they could ship the wine to her.

"How long will it take to arrive?" she asked.

"Only a week or so. It will come directly to you."

She also paid the shipping cost; all was set. She was already looking forward to receiving her special package from Germany shortly after she returned home.

The organizing of the wine order put my sister in a slightly better mood than she had been that day so far. Because of The Baltic Plague setting her sinuses running amok, she went through an entire box of Kleenex in the hour we spent at the winery.

Our next stop was Leiwen, roughly half the distance back to Trier. She had met a German fellow named Andreas Bender at the fancy schmancy dinner/wine festival in Edmonton at a restaurant that no longer exists. Andreas was in Canada promoting his wines, and he attended this dinner, providing the wines and pairing them with the food. It was a ten-course meal. She was impressed with his wines at this dinner and was on the hunt for him and his wine in Germany.

"He's really good-looking. And he makes great wine. We have to go check his place out," she told me.

Good-looking and great wine. Okay.

She had an address, but we drove around in circles for several minutes after arriving in Leiwen, not sure where we were supposed to stop. Leiwen is not a big place. In fact, The Googler indicates it is a municipality—not even a town. The population as of December 1, 2019, was 1,547.[19]

There was nothing anywhere in the vicinity that the GPS took us that looked like a winery. Finally, we stopped where the GPS directed us—a residential building we had driven past three times. And we were at the right spot. It appeared Andreas made and bottled his wines in his garage. It was actually a workshop, but from the street, it looked like his garage, and what was obviously his house was right beside it.

We walked into the "garage."

"Hello?" my sister called out.

A handsome young man in his thirties with brown hair and bright blue eyes emerged from behind some massive wine-making equipment.

"Hi, I'm Janice. We met in Edmonton a few months ago."

"Ah, yes." He remembered the event and meeting her.

This was Andreas Bender, the owner of the winery. And apparently he fulfilled every other staff role as well.

He gave us the tour, which involved showing us around the single room, telling us what each piece of equipment was for. And my sister asked about his wines.

I largely tuned out at this point. I like wine, but I have no desire to be an expert who can spout off about blackberry and coffee and notes of this and that. There are types of reds I like and others that I don't. Likewise with white. And I'm happy to spend what it takes to get a decent bottle of wine. But I don't put any effort into pairing wine with whatever I happen to be eating. I just open a bottle of Whatever I Feel Like Drinking, vintage Whenever It Was Made.

But his wines were really good, so I bought a couple of bottles of them to take home.

My sister was still sick at this point; her antibiotics hadn't fully cured her yet. Her symptoms were different from mine. I had suffered through severe sinus pain and congestion and a relentless, hacking cough. She describes her version of The Baltic Plague as a massive head cold—the worst head cold of her life—and the worst day of her plague was that day when she went through an entire box of Kleenex at Dr. Loosen's winery.

***

From Leiwen to Trier is a thirty-minute drive, so we easily made our trips to Janice's chosen wineries over the course of one day.

What else was there to do in that area?

Karl Marx was from Trier. The town is home to Karl Marx House—the building where Marx was born, which was opened as a museum in May 1947. We decided we needed to go there, but we also quickly made an almost unspoken agreement that we wouldn't tour the museum since neither of us are museum buffs. We went inside the lobby, saw that the entrance had a bronze bust of Marx and a gift shop, and decided that would be the extent of our Marxist tour. We snapped photos with the bust and perused the tiny gift shop. I bought a "Christmas tree ornament" and nothing else. I'm still not even sure if that's what this item is supposed to be. It's a small doll in the image of Karl Marx made of felt and with a loop on the top so that it can be hung somewhere. I figured it was meant to be a Christmas tree ornament. I mean, nothing says Christmas like Karl Marx hanging on the Christmas tree, right?

And after all, the Germans, at least in my mind, hang weird objects on their Christmas trees. It was the Germans who introduced the rest of the world to the idea of hanging lights on the Christmas tree, except in the early days, the "lights" were real candles. I'm sure they looked lovely, but I also imagine how much of a fire hazard they presented. Over time, the candles were replaced with electric lights, and many of us adopted the inverted tear-drop shaped bulbs that we string on our trees, likely without knowing the origin of this tradition.

But wait; there's more. The Germans didn't stop there.

In 2003, before my first trip to Germany, Dave, a friend in Calgary, gave me a strange little plastic Christmas ornament. It was in the shape and colour of a pickle, and it had a button on it which, after being pressed, would prompt the pickle ornament to break out in song. Namely a yodel.

The explanation on the box explained that this was a traditional German Christmas ornament (okay, maybe not the yodelling part). According to the story on the box, a pickle was traditionally hung on the Christmas tree and was part of a children's game. Whichever child found the pickle ornament first would get a prize. The game was a challenge being as the pickle blended into the tree.

Of course I thought this yodelling pickle was hysterical, and I hang it on my tree every year despite having no children in my house for Christmas. The only prize anyone has ever gotten is the privilege of pushing the button to initiate the spectacular yodelling.

Six years after I received the Precious Pickle, Christine and Alan were visiting me for a couple of weeks. Their visit coincided with my birthday, so I organized a small dinner with the two of them, Alex (my co-worker who had been born and raised in Munich), and a few other friends, including Dave, the friend who had given me the pickle. Over dinner, the conversation turned to The Holy Pickle.

"What's the story with the Christmas pickle?" my friend Dave asked Christine.

"What's a Christmas pickle?" she replied.

"You know, the pickle ornament that you Germans hang on the Christmas tree. And then whichever kid finds it gets a prize. How did that tradition start?"

"I have no idea what you're talking about!" Christine laughed.

"Maybe it's a Bavarian thing," I said. "Christine's from Saxony. Maybe they only do this in the south. Do you know the origin of this tradition?" I asked Alex, my co-worker who had been born in Munich.

He let loose a great belly laugh. "I've never heard of this either."

"That's not possible!" I said. "I bought glass pickle Christmas ornaments in a store the first time I was in Munich! It's obviously a custom in Germany!"

Both Christine and Alex were adamant they had never heard of this tradition before. Neither of them had ever hung pickles (glass or real, singing or otherwise) on their Christmas trees.

"I think you guys are just too embarrassed to admit this is one of your traditions!" Dave said as we all laughed and changed the topic.

I *had* bought some glass pickle ornaments the first time I was in Germany. Mom and I were shopping in some of the stores around Marienplatz in Munich—stores that offered hand-crafted cuckoo clocks, nutcrackers, linens, and glass ornaments. In one store I found some glass tree ornaments and debated for several minutes which set of ornaments to buy for my friend Kara, who is an associate pastor at a Baptist church: the nativity scene ornaments or the pickles. I knew the nativity scene would be appropriate and she would love them, but Kara is one of the silliest people I know. I opted for the pickles and, upon giving them to her that Christmas, had to explain to her this German tradition that all of the real Germans in my life deny.

***

I'm up for wacky adventures just to say I did them. Anyone who has read my book *Living My Golden Dream* will have learned about the time I went to Singapore on a five-day trip: Day One was travel, as was Day Five. Day Two was spent touring Singapore. Day Three saw me and my travel companion hop a bus and cross the border into Malaysia, where we spent the afternoon. And on Day Four, we went south, taking a ferry to Batam Island, part of Indonesia. Since Singapore is small and we covered everything we wanted to see in one day, we took advantage of the opportunity to get two additional stamps in our passports by spending each day in a different country. Three days, three countries. Some parts of Asia and Europe allow for those types of opportunities.

Thus was the case when Janice and I were in Trier. We noticed that Trier was less than a one-hour drive from the city of Luxembourg, in … the itty-bitty country of the same name.

I knew precisely nothing about Luxembourg except that it's not a big place. Like Singapore.

Wine, Bach, and Cuckoo Clocks

I now know that Luxembourg has three official languages: French, German, and Luxembourgish. Yes, that last one is apparently real. But until I went there, I didn't know much about this speck on the map.

While in our hotel room in Trier, we decided that we were done with that area—we had visited the wineries on my sister's list and gotten a sufficient dose of Marxism. We concurred that we needed to head to Luxembourg, just to say we'd been there.

"Why don't we drive there, stay overnight, and them come back?" I suggested. "That way we can truly say we've been there if we've spent one night there."

"Sure, let's do that," Janice said.

I got onto Hotels.com and saw that hotel rooms in Luxembourg were pricey. However, I had credit in my Hotels.com account.

"Hey, I can get us a room at a five-star hotel for six bucks!" I announced.

"What? How?"

"I have a $320 credit to use on Hotels.com, and a room at this swanky hotel is $326. I say let's do it. If we're going to Luxembourg, we might as well stay in style."

"Okay, works for me," she said.

"Cool. I'll book a room and then you'll owe me three bucks."

The landscape consisted of rolling hills, lots of greenery with plentiful trees. The highway was in great shape and was nice to drive. I did feel like we were in a different country, even just driving the highway.

I was immediately struck by how clean, bright, and modern the city looked—at least the part of the city we were in.

My sister loves fine dining, and in particular, French food. Since we were in a country with French influence, she wanted a French meal.

When we sat down at our table, the server presented us with menus ... in French.

"Ok, you're up," I said. "Up to now, I've been fumbling my way trying to translate for you with my weak knowledge of German. You studied French, but I never did. Your turn to translate for me."

She struggled a bit as she hadn't used her French language skills in eons, but she did manage to translate most of the menu items for me.

We partook of a delicious French meal: escargot, pork tenderloin with bacon and apple Riesling sauce, sole meunière, and great wine. We slept well in our fancy schmancy hotel, got up the next morning, and drove back to Germany.

So yeah, I've been to Luxembourg. For dinner. And a good sleep.

***

Oh, and that case of Dr. Loosen wine my sister got shipped … I need to explain how *that* all ended.

We returned from Germany and my sister waited for her special box of liquid loveliness. When writing the first draft of this book, I asked her to relay to me her version of The Wine Debacle:

"I've been all over the world, just like you have, and I gather wine: Italy, Australia, New Zealand, California, France. Numerous times I've brought my wine back with me as checked baggage on the plane. This time, they convinced me that I didn't need to do that. 'Oh yeah, we're good. We're gonna send this to you. We have shipping protocols we have blabbidy blabbidy blah blah blah' and I believed them. They told me that when it arrives, it'll all be intact. Everything would be fine, and I didn't have to pay any more, blah blee blah. I bring usually two cases as checked baggage, and I have to pay extra but it's still worth it 'cause it's amazing wine that you're never gonna get anywhere in Canada.

"So for whatever reason I decided to trust these crazy Germans. Remember, we brought a case of Andreas Bender's wine back as checked baggage and it was fine, which is my experience. Dr. Loosen wine, not so much because they were shipping it to us.

"I don't know how, but it got frozen. I think once airplanes get to a certain altitude if they don't put cargo in the proper part of the aircraft, it'll freeze.

"And then it sat in Ontario for two freaking weeks and who knows what happened to it there, but anyway, eventually we got our money back from Dr. Loosen because they realized they messed up astronomically. When I got the wine, all the corks had popped out. We did get a refund, but that's not the point. We wanted the wine. Never never again."

"Wasn't there some sort of fiasco with also trying to find out where it was for a few weeks, too?" I asked.

"Oh God, yeah. I got on the phone trying to track it down. And I was given the royal runaround between the winery, who said it was in Canada, and Canadian Customs and Immigration, who said it hadn't arrived yet. Nobody knew where it was.

"If I want wine, I just know now to bring it as checked baggage, bring it through Alberta, and pay whatever duty they charge."

Christmas in the Nick of Time

Since childhood, one of my life goals was to spend Christmas in Germany at least once. When I was a child, my family had our own Christmas traditions, as every family does, but as I got older, into late elementary school and junior high school, I realized that our traditions were different from those of many of my friends.

Although we were not Lutheran, there were scads of people in the church my family attended (The Evangelical Church of Canada) who had German ancestry, so some of the traditions in our church were similar to those in the Lutheran church. My childhood was influenced by the traditions of my grandparents and the other people in the church of my parents' and grandparents' generations. Particularly at Christmastime, I always felt like I had an extended family at church, as it was a close-knit community, and the Christmas services and children's pageants were a time of close fellowship, celebration—and of course candy.

The older I got, the more I started to wonder how close our Christmas traditions were to those of a "real" German family in Germany.

So in 2014, when it was my turn to visit Christine, I checked with her if it would be alright if I spent Christmas and New Year with her and her family. It was absolutely okay, so I booked my flights, including a three-day detour in Munich before arriving in Leipzig on the evening of the 24th. I made sure I would arrive early enough on the 24th so as not to disrupt their plans for Christmas Eve, and I wanted to be there to spend this evening with my friends. To me, Christmas is the 24th.

My father had a stroke in October that year and was in the hospital for the three months leading up to Christmas. It was a stressful time, what with his recovery and not knowing what the long-term impact would be on him. Janice and I were already realizing that his days of driving a vehicle were over, and of course we greatly struggled with how to broach that subject with him. (Fortunately the doctors made the decision for us and informed him of his new status.)

But we didn't know what his life would look like other than he seemed to be recovering well but would need to continue physio and mental exercises to keep progressing. During his time in the hospital, I had been there almost every day, a one-hour drive from my home, and many times I made that drive twice a day, depending on his therapy and which specialists were attending to him on any given day.

By the time my trip to Germany rolled around, he had been discharged from the hospital for two weeks and we had found him new living arrangements. He was settling in well. I felt guilty about not being with him for Christmas that year, but I knew my sister would be spending Christmas with him, and I badly needed a break. Off to Munich to take in the Christmas markets for a few days before heading north to celebrate Christmas with my friends.

***

One item on my to-do list was to check out some Christmas markets in Germany. Munich's market at Marienplatz, the main square in front of the Rathaus (town hall), where visitors can take in the famed Glockenspiel, is supposedly the most original and authentic market in Munich. My hotel was within walking distance of Marienplatz, so I easily made my way to the market to meander about, do some shopping, and enjoy some Glühwein, the traditional mulled wine that is popular in Germany at Christmas.

Glühwein translates to "glow wine," and the name derives "from the red hot [sic] irons used to heat the wine across Germanic cultures when the drink first became popular hundreds of years ago."[20] At the markets, friends gather in the evening, mingling with each other and strangers over a glass or two or three of Glühwein. I bought some Christmas ornaments and although I was alone, I took in the festive atmosphere and the joviality of the locals mingling and enjoying some drinks. I laughed at the model of a bigger-than-life-sized pig advertising the sausage booth and tried some of their offerings. Yum.

The next day, I did a bit of shopping in Marienplatz before heading to the airport. I bought myself a Christmas present—something I had for years been yearning for: a green silk Dirndl.

My one-hour flight to Leipzig was scheduled to depart at 4 pm, so I arrived at the airport an hour before departure and went to check in at the self-serve kiosk. I scanned my passport, entered my flight number, and ... nothing.

Hmm. Strange.

I let the machine reset and tried again.

After three attempts and receiving the message three times that my flight was not available, I checked the paper printout I had brought with me of my itinerary. Yep. I had all the information correct, but the kiosk was not finding my flight for some reason. I approached the Lufthansa desk, handed the printout of my itinerary to the agent, and gave her my passport.

"Hello. I'm having trouble checking in for my flight. Could you help me?"

She typed away at her computer and, after a couple of minutes, informed me that the problem was that I had missed my flight.

"The flight you are booked on is going to take off in five minutes, and it is no longer possible to get on it."

"What? Air Canada sent me several revisions to my itinerary, but this printout shows the most recent information they sent."

Nope. The flight was departing momentarily.

"Is there *any* way I could get on the flight?"

Nein. They had closed the gate.

"You will have to phone Air Canada and rebook your flight. I cannot rebook it for you."

Phone Air Canada? I had visions of being given the supreme run around and being on the phone for hours. Even if I got hold of a real person, I had zero faith that I was going to get any help.

Without warning, taking her off guard and surprising myself even more, I burst into tears. Fat, slobbering, blubbery tears. Snot pouring out of my nose. I was wailing loudly and uncontrollably, and I lit off.

"I'm sorry [*sniff*]. I know this isn't your fault, and I'm not trying to be difficult, but I thought I had the most recent information out of all of the changes they made. I know I printed out the most recent email they sent me. My dad had a stroke in October, and it's just been a really stressful few months, and I'm heading to Leipzig to spend Christmas with my good friend who lives there and we've been good friends for more than fifteen years and I wanted to spend Christmas with her and especially with all the stress I've been under the past few months, I just really need to get there tonight [*sniff*] and now I don't know what to do. WAAAAHHHHH!"

I wasn't trying to be manipulative. I had simply snapped. All of the stress of having dealt with my dad's stroke less then four years after losing my mom had finally caught up with me after bottling it all up.

She started typing again.

"I can get you to Leipzig tonight on the last flight from Frankfurt. You will have to fly from here to Frankfurt and then have a three-hour layover in Frankfurt before catching the last flight out to Leipzig tonight. The flight to Frankfurt leaves in an hour."

"Really?" [*sniff*]

I had had visions of madly trying to catch a train from Munich to Leipzig, arriving God-knows-when, and not knowing if I would even find a seat. Being that it was Christmas Eve, surely half the country was on the move and the trains would be jam packed.

"Oh thank you so much! That would be fine!" I told her. She booked me on the flights, no charge, handed me my boarding passes, and wished me a Merry Christmas. I thanked her three more times and told her I was so greatly appreciative of her help. I wished her a Merry Christmas and set out to get through security and to my gate, where I texted Christine and told her I was on the milk run.

"I've taken that flight many times from Frankfurt," she replied. "It's not only the last flight to Leipzig for the day; it's the last flight out of the airport for the night and it feels like they are kicking you out of town," she told me. "See you when you get here."

***

Christine was at the Leipzig airport to meet me.

"I was on my way to pick you up earlier when I got your message that you had missed your flight, so I had some time to kill. I invited myself over to a friend's house for a drink rather than going back home and coming again to pick you up."

She didn't seem too bothered that I had disrupted her schedule, and she took me home.

"Alan isn't home yet. He'll be back in a couple of hours, but his company sent his Christmas hamper today."

Alan is a pilot and Christine jokes that she is a "war bride" because he is sometimes gone for days at a time.

"I may never get to see my husband, but at least I get a great Christmas hamper out of the deal!" She laughed as she picked up the hamper from the table. "I waited to open it until you arrived."

She tore into the box and started to pull items out. Cookies, Stollen (traditional German Christmas cake), wine, another bottle of wine, some cheese. I decided I liked the idea of a business or company giving their employees a Christmas hamper.

Yet another foreign tradition that Canada needs to adopt.

Alan arrived home shortly after Christine had opened the hamper, and the three of us enjoyed a few drinks and some laughs before calling it a night.

Christmas-day lunch was beef tongue (another German treat that I had loved since growing up on the farm, where we butchered our own beef), after which we packed up and went to Christine's brother's house an hour away. The three of us, along with Christine's parents, would be staying with Markus (her brother) and his wife (Annett) and two daughters (Sarah and Julia) for a few days.

Christine ushered me to my room—one of the girls' rooms. After I settled my suitcase in the room and went downstairs to join the family, the first order of business was for the girls, who were twelve and six at the time, to shyly settle themselves in front of me, smiles on their faces, and tell me in English, "We have a present for you."

The oldest passed me a handmade card with pictures drawn on the front and a note inside, "We want to wish you a Merry Christmas" in English. They had both signed their names. What a treasured gift!

I've spent lots of time with Christine's family. There's always the beloved cake and coffee in the late afternoon, during which everyone gathers to socialize and indulge in some of Germany's incomparable cakes. In the afternoon, since the weather was pleasant, we all went for a walk. Christine's brother lives in the country, on the outskirts of the nearest town. The houses aren't far from one another, but there are plenty of fields and pastureland surrounding them. We made our way through the neighbourhood at one point stopping so that Alan could have a Christmas-day chat with a mild-mannered, friendly-looking cow. After our walk, it was time for cake and coffee.

And because of cake and coffee time at 4 pm, dinner is later, in true European style. Germans, as is the case with other Europeans, know how to properly enjoy their evening meals. The mealtime is a couple of hours long; families gather at the end of the day to relax, enjoy the food and company without rushing to down the meal and get somewhere else. There are always tons of great food and wine.

After dinner, once the girls had scuttled off to play without the adults, we sat around the table to take in their evening tradition. Every dinner I've had with Christine's family has been followed by whiskey and conversation well into the late hours. My German isn't great, but I listen and try to catch what I can. It's rare that I contribute to the conversation because as poor as my listening skills are, they are better than my speaking skills. I manage to usually catch the gist of the conversation, and once in a while, Alan translates a bit for me.

The next day, Christine and Markus were determined to find some culture for me nearby. They decided they would take me on the Abenteuer Bergwerk mine tour in the Erzgebirge, a mountainous area along the Czech border which was mined over centuries for silver, tin, zinc, cobalt, nickel, copper, and uranium. We were the only visitors at the time we were there, perhaps the only ones that day; the woman working there seemed thrilled to have customers, and we donned yellow plastic rain ponchos and blue hard hats to protect ourselves from the moisture and rocky walls within the mine. The forty-five minute tour took us through some narrow tunnels and entryways between the open spaces. The walls were seeping, and the mine was humid. Lights guided our path in most places, but some sections were dark. We memorialized the outing with a silly picture of the four of us (Alan, Christine, Markus, and me) in our lovely outfits, all grinning.

Between Christmas and New Year, we went back to Leipzig and spent our time relaxing, going for walks, watching movies, and sitting around the dining room table or living room chatting. I had come to

Germany wanting to experience Christmas and in particular the Christmas markets. At one point during my visit, I said to Christine, "I thought there would be more variety of handicrafts and Christmas ornaments and such at the Christmas market. There were some kiosks with those, but there were a lot more stands for beer and Glühwein."

"The Christmas markets aren't for shopping! They are for drinking!" she informed me, laughing at my naïveté.

***

One of the highlights of my visit that year was New Year's Eve.

Several of Alan's colleagues—other pilots from Belgium, Wales, and Spain—were in Leipzig over New Year, so Alan invited them to come and spend the evening with us. Each of them brought a bottle of wine, and I was surprised to see the Spanish pilot show up with a bottle of one of my favourite wines that I buy at home. It's hard to find in Calgary, but I do know a couple of stores that carry it. I told him how much I enjoyed the wine, and he seemed pleased and surprised that a Canadian recognized his contribution to the evenings' festivities.

I was starting to get sick by then; I had a sinus cold coming on, but I was determined to ring in the new year, so I toughed it out. We spent the evening around the table drinking wine, having snacks, and playing card games. At one point I needed to use the bathroom, so I went upstairs and opened the door of the bathroom to find one of the male guests standing at the toilet. I hadn't noticed that anyone else had left the table.

"Ach! Entschuldigung!" I apologized.

Just then Christine came up the stairs.

"Jaysus! What is it with you people? There's a lock on the door!" She laughed and chastised us.

A few days earlier, I had been in the bathroom using the toilet and hadn't locked the door either. Alan walked in on me and apologized profusely, embarrassed as he was. I assured him it was my fault for not locking the door. Christine was befuddled as to why no one used the lock on the door of her damn guest bathroom. (Also, when we were staying at Markus's house, I walked in on Annett in the bathroom while she was doing her hair; she hadn't locked the door either!)

Wine, Bach, and Cuckoo Clocks

What I have never admitted to Christine after multiple visits to Germany over almost twenty-five years is that I am forever stumped by the doors and windows in Germany. The locking mechanisms on them are different than they are in Canada and the US, and I am forever twisting and turning and turning back and turning some more and listening for a click but no, that's not the right click, so I need to turn and twist some more for the other type of click and do the hokey pokey to try and open a door or window. The reason I wasn't locking the door in her bathroom was my fear of locking myself in. I have always thought that would be more embarrassing and much more likely than having someone walk in on me when I was on the toilet.

I'm always excited to chat with people from other cultures and learn about their countries and cities. The conversation on New Year's Eve distracted me enough that I hadn't considered what the midnight hour would bring. I had assumed that the group of us would raise our glasses around the table, do the countdown, and wish each other a happy new year. I was in for a surprise and a treat.

Fifteen minutes to midnight, we heard pops and bangs coming from the streets. I looked at Christine quizzingly, and she smiled.

"The neighbours are beginning to celebrate early," she said. "Well, shall we get our coats and join them?"

We all donned our jackets and went out into the street, where twenty people were already gathered, many of whom were setting off fireworks.

I had had no idea that the custom in Germany on New Year's Eve was to flock to the streets and set off fireworks for an hour. Two? However long the weather and supply of fireworks would permit. For me, this was an exciting and novel experience. For Christine, it was just another normal New Year's Eve, except she and Alan had several guests for the evening.

Christine and Alan warned me not to get too close so that I wouldn't get hit with one of the crackers. When the countdown began, and firecrackers blasted around us, we all hugged and kissed, raised our glasses of wine. We remained in the street for twenty minutes as the firecrackers got louder and louder.

Christine and Alan live near the Leipzig Zoo, so one of the bonuses of visiting them is that we can go for walks together in the park that is adjacent to the zoo and sometimes catch a glimpse of giraffes, hippos, or other zoo residents. On January 1, we went for a walk in the park, and while we saw a few animals, the main sight was the abundant garbage on the ground: streamers, tubes, and firecracker coverings littering the pathways and the grass. Yes, 2015 came in with a bang.

***

I tend to hoard, collect, acquire, whatever you want to call it. I inherited this trait from my mother, who held onto years' worth of *Good Housekeeping* magazines, recipes she had cut out of various other magazines, Tupperware, twist ties, jars, bottles, rags, other scraps of cloth, buttons, zippers she had torn out of clothes before discarding said clothes (or turning them into aforementioned rags). You name it, she held onto it because she "might need it someday."

Christmas in Germany was also a treat for me in that I wasn't surrounded by clutter, noise (other than the firecrackers), busyness, stress, and "stuff." I was pleasantly surprised to see that while a lot of houses and other buildings were decorated, the decorations were mostly limited to lights. And the lights were all natural; there were very few blues, greens, or reds anywhere and even fewer Santas, reindeer, snowmen, and other images. After visiting my father in the hospital every day for three months following his stroke, the simplicity of the lights and their colour—or lack thereof—in Germany was calming and comforting for me. The decorations, coupled with spending time with my friend and her family just being, allowed me to catch my breath.

In Search of David

I had travelled to my ancestors' homeland with my mother, my friends, and then my sister, so on solo trips, starting in 2010, I began to add on another country most times I went to Germany. I figured that was a good way to check other parts of Europe off my list while I was in the area. My side trip to Poland was full of great food, history, and learning and left me eager to explore more of Europe. My next trip after spending Christmas in Germany brought me another opportunity—one I didn't see coming.

Ten months after my dad had his stroke, I struck up a conversation with my dad—one that I had been dreading.

"I think we need to sell your truck."

Silence. My dad was a man of few words at the best of times, but he also needed a lot of thinking time before making a decision—one of the many traits I inherited from him.

"No one is driving it," I told him. "I had to boost it to get it running again, and if it sits in front of my house for a long time without being driven, we'll have to boost it again."

I didn't want to remind him he would never drive again. Nurses, occupational therapists, physiotherapists, and a doctor had told him as so, but he was still holding out hope. It was obvious, though, that his abilities were not going to improve enough for him to ever drive again. Instead, I tried appealing to his sense of frugality.

"The longer the truck sits, the less it will be worth. I think if we sell it now, we'll get a good price for it."

He drew in a long, deep breath.

"Ok. I guess so," he said.

Janice, Dad, and I discussed various options and decided to put Dad's truck in the farm equipment auction that an auction house was having a few weeks later. She drove Dad's truck and followed me on the highway. When we got to the auction house, we went into the office to take care of the business side of things: filling out the paperwork, leaving a copy of the registration and insurance, and borrowing a wrench so we could remove the license plate. We took care of everything and then piled into my vehicle to make the forty-five minute drive back to Airdrie, where I was living.

Janice was in the back seat of my SUV, Dad was in the passenger seat, and of course, I was driving. My sister was on her cell phone checking text messages, perusing the Internet, and chattering to us.

"Oh. I've been meaning to ask you," she said at one point, "do you know someone named Marina Bartolozzi?"

"Holy cow, yes! That was my Italian pen pal when I was a teenager, but we lost touch years ago. Why?" I replied.

"She messaged me through Facebook looking for you."

"Oh wow, really?"

"Yeah, but I didn't respond to her yet. I didn't know if you knew who she was and if you'd want me to give her your contact information in case it's a scammer or something."

"No, if it's truly her, I'd definitely love to get in touch with her!"

"Ok, I'll show you her profile picture on Facebook when we get back to your house and you can contact her if you want to. It's the one with the cat profile picture." She laughed.

"Oh. Hard to tell then if it's really her." I laughed in return.

When we got to my house, I took my sister's phone from her and poked around a bit, looking into the account. Based on the information I could see and what my gut was telling me, I was confident this was my long-lost friend.

And so I sent a friend request.

***

When I was a teenager, I had pen pals from all over the world: Finland, Germany (West Germany at the time), Egypt, South Korea, Australia, and Italy. I wrote faithfully to all of them for several years, but we all lost touch along the way as we finished high school and moved forward with our adult lives.

Marina was the one I had kept in touch with the longest and felt the closest to. She grew up in Rome with her twin sister and parents. At one point during my junior high school years, I wanted to go to Italy and meet her in person, but my parents couldn't afford to send me on such a faraway, expensive trip, so I resigned myself to maybe going to Italy "someday." Throughout our teenage years, Marina had sent me pictures of herself as a young girl in her ballet lessons and current pictures of herself and her friends on school trips to Tuscany and Pisa.

She also sent me a postcard of the statue of *David* ... such a scandalous piece of paper for me, a twelve-year old small-town girl whose mother dragged me to church every Sunday. Young as I was, I didn't giggle and titter over David's nakedness, though. Instead, I marvelled at the beauty of this piece of marble and imagined going to see it with my own eyes one day, knowing that other artistic masterpieces were in that same part of the world.

I don't remember exactly when or how Marina and I lost touch with each other. It was sometime around my university graduation when I was in transition, living at a camp in the mountains for the summer and then moving back to my parents' place while I waited for my work visa for Japan.

I don't know why I didn't write her from Japan once I knew my mailing address there. I can only chalk it up to being scatterbrained and overwhelmed at a significant life change—moving for a minimum of two years across the planet from everything and everyone I had ever known.

***

After I sent the Facebook friend request, Janice left, and I took my dad home. With the time difference between Canada and Italy, I wasn't expecting a response, if any, until the next day at the earliest.

That evening, my friend Lisa and I were attending the Dolly Parton concert in Calgary. We met for dinner and then walked to the Saddledome for the concert. Dolly was everything she should have been and more, and roughly halfway through the show was an intermission.

When intermission began, Lisa and I chatted for a few moments and then we both checked our phones for messages.
I had two new messages from Facebook:

1. Marina Bartolozzi has accepted your friend request.
2. "Hello Lorna!!! I'm so happy to hear from you!!!" from Marina through Facebook Messenger.

For the rest of the intermission, Marina and I messaged each other in real time.

"I'm crying right now, I'm so happy to be reunited with you!" she messaged me.

"I'm at a concert right now. It's 8 pm here. I have a few minutes that I can chat with you. I'm so excited to reconnect with you!"

"I wish we could meet one day!" she said.

"I have good friends in Germany, and we visit each other every year, either here in Canada or there in Germany. Next year is my turn to go to Germany, so maybe I should try to stop in Italy on the same trip and we could meet each other!"

I started to think about stopping in Rome for a couple of days to meet this woman I'd had no contact with for thirty years but who sounded exactly like my vivacious, funny, lovely childhood friend.

"Yes! That would be wonderful!" she replied.

"Ok, let's see if it will work!" I told her.

Over the next several months, we connected every week or two on Messenger, updating each other on the thirty years of our lives that we had missed. She was married and had a daughter, and she still lived in Rome. I was not married, and I had not had any children. She said she'd been looking for me off and on for several years but could never find anything about me on the Internet.

After several chats, she revealed the breakthrough she'd had.

"I want to tell you how I found your sister and why I reached out to her instead of to you."

"Ok." I waited to hear her explanation.

"I could never find anything about you until one day I tried again, and I found your mom's obituary. I saw your name on there, so I searched for you again on Facebook, but I couldn't find you. Then I saw your sister's name in the obituary, and I remembered you telling me when we were teenagers that you had a sister. I was sure that was her, so I sent her a message."

"Ah, I keep my Facebook account private because as a high school teacher, I don't want my students to find me and send me friend requests. But my sister told me about your message, so that's how I knew to contact you here!"

"I'm so glad she did!"

So was I. And I now had a perfect excuse to go to Italy.

***

The next year in August, I took a three-week vacation: two weeks in Italy and one in Germany.

I stepped off the plane in Rome knowing that a driver from my hotel would be meeting me. I wasn't going to stay with Marina. She had offered, but I was a little unsure being that we had never met in person. I didn't want to be an annoying, messy, intrusive guest. Plus, she fosters cats, and I'm allergic to cats. A hotel seemed like a good idea to give us both our space.

I looked around at the airport and saw no one carrying a sign with my name on it.

I wandered but I didn't want to go too far. I stuck to the area where there were people waiting for incoming passengers.

After I walked back and forth three times, I finally saw a young man holding a sign with my name on it.

I almost had to pick my jaw up off the ground.

This man, in his early thirties by my best guess, had thick, black Italian hair, wavy and perfectly styled. He was wearing what was clearly an expensive suit and shoes and was movie-star gorgeous. I looked around to make sure he was indeed waiting for me. Yep.

He greeted me with a hello and picked up my suitcase, carrying it outside to his Mercedes.

After he placed my suitcase in the trunk, he popped on a pair of expensive-looking aviator sunglasses, opened the car door for me, and then slid into the driver's seat. I spent the next forty minutes trying not to stare at him *too* much.

I've been in Italy less than an hour and already everything is an impressive stereotype.

Wine, Bach, and Cuckoo Clocks

We arrived at the hotel close to noon. Marina was at work until the end of the afternoon, so I snuggled into bed for a good long nap.

When I woke up, I had a shower, put on some clean clothes, and went down to the lobby to wait for my friend. She had texted me to say she was on her way, so I settled into a chair.

After ten minutes, I heard the front door open.

I saw a woman approach the desk and start to speak, in Italian of course, to the clerk, who gestured in my direction. The woman turned her head and then froze. For a moment she stood motionless, and then she put one of her hands upon her mouth as if to silence herself.

I broke out into a huge smile, walked up, and gave her a hug.

It was as if we were old friends meeting after a long separation. Indeed, that's what we were.

***

Marina was working the next few days, so I toured myself around Rome. The night that I arrived, she took me to see the Trevi Fountain before we had dinner, so as I explored other sights in the city, I saw it in daylight, as well. I checked other main attractions off the list: the Spanish Steps, the Pantheon, Vittorio Emanuele II Monument, Palatine Hill, and Piazza Navona.

Everything was a highlight because I'm a huge history and especially archaeology buff, but the tour I did of the Colosseum and my self-guided walk through the Forum were my favourite experiences. I paid for the VIP tour of the Colosseum, which took us to the lower level, where the animal cages were. When we had a bit of free time at the end of the guided tour, I climbed into the seating area, sat down, and imagined what it would have been like to be a spectator in this unique and spectacular setting. I thought back to the movie *Gladiator* and imagined the roaring crowd cheering during the fights.

I then wandered over to the Forum.

Walking on the stones that were carved with grooves from chariot wheels, reminding myself that I was walking on the same stones where Julius Caesar had walked, left me dumbfounded. I had recently seen Shakespeare's *Julius Caesar* performed in Calgary by The Shakespeare Company, so thoughts of his demise were fresh in my mind as I walked through the stone streets. I imagined all of the bloodshed during the wars and battles in Roman history. The fight for power, the backstabbing, the horses, even the clothing. I felt the same sense of awe I felt when I had set foot on the Great Wall of China and stood in Zeppelin Park in Nuremburg years earlier; I kept reminding myself that I was truly walking in a place I had only seen in the movies and in documentaries—a place I had studied and had imagined visiting.

When I got to the top of the Vittoriano (a large monument built to honour Victor Emmanuel II, the first king of Italy) on the Capitoline Hill, where the views above the Forum and the Colosseum are clear and wide, I decided to share some of this jaw-dropping history with folks at home. I did a short Facebook live video, explaining and showing the view of the Forum below me and the awe I was filled with to be standing there.

I put my phone in my pocket and started chatting with a young fellow, an Asian American who was also there for the first time.

"It's just incredible, isn't it?"

"Amazing," he replied.

"I only arrived yesterday and already I feel like I've gotten my money's worth out of the plane ticket."

He laughed. "Yeah, the history here is so deep and so rich."

"I know. I'm from Canada, and my province had their hundredth anniversary a few years ago. When I told my friend from Germany about the celebrations, she laughed at me and said, 'You have no idea what history is until you visit Europe.'"

He laughed again. "Which part of Canada are you from?"

"I live near Calgary, a couple hours north of the Montana border."

"Oh nice. I live in San Francisco."

"Ah, I love San Francisco! It's one of my favourite cities."

We chatted for several minutes until he decided to move on.

"Well, enjoy your vacation!" he said as he walked away.

"You too!"

I took a few pictures, and then I went onto Facebook to see if anyone had commented on my video.

Erm. Most of the comments were on the video I hadn't realized I was taking. Seems I had unknowingly left my phone recording while the young man and I were chatting, and the comments were flying in.

"Are you bringing him home with you?"

"Look at you! You haven't even been in Italy for two days and you're already picking up men!"

"Good for you—chatting up the boys!"

I joined the chat.

"Pu-leez!! WE WERE JUST TALKING! He seemed like a nice young man, and we were both so awestruck by the view!"

"Yeah, and what was the view like beside you?"

I rolled my eyes, laughed, pocketed my phone again, and carried on with my self-guided tour.

***

Once I had seen the sights of Rome and Marina was off work on her August vacation days, she, her daughter, and I boarded a train and headed north. I stayed at Abano Terme, a spa resort town a forty-five-minute train ride south of Venice, while Marina stayed with her husband, who lived and worked in the next town over. From Abano Terme, I took day trips to Venice as well as to the small city of Padua, where I was lucky enough to get a last-minute walk-in ticket to visit the Scrovengi Chapel, home of Tuscan painter Giotto's greatest fresco, painted between 1303-1305. (There are benefits to travelling solo! Getting a single ticket to events and attractions at the last minute is sometimes pretty easy.)

Marina, her daughter, and I also took a day trip to Verona. As a high school English teacher, I could certainly not get that close to Verona, the city of Shakespeare's *Romeo and Juliet*, without a visit. Marina found someone to give us a private tour of the castle (Castelvecchio), Lamberti's Tower, and of course, Juliet's House, which was expectedly swarming with people. I took a few shots of the statue of Juliet in the courtyard to discover later that one of my photos captured only the hand of someone reaching up toward the statue; in the photo, it looked like this person was reaching up to caress the statue's right boob. Many tourists rub the statue's right breast because it is said that doing so will bring that person good luck in love. (In 2024, the right breast developed a hole in it—and not for the first time—from so many people rubbing it.) We ended our day in Verona at the open-air market, where I couldn't resist buying a couple of cheap, tacky *Romeo and Juliet* themed T-shirts.

The three of us returned to Verona a few days later with Marina's husband to attend an opera. Arena di Verona Festival is the annual summer opera festival held at the Verona Arena, a Roman amphitheatre similar in appearance to but much smaller than the Colosseum in Rome. The festival features several shows throughout summer. We opted to see *Madame Butterfly* on the last night we were in the area. The next day, I was moving on to spend a few days in Florence by myself before returning to Rome to again meet up with Marina after she also returned home.

Prior to attending *Madame Butterfly*, I had only been to two operas, both in Calgary. Admittedly, I don't like opera—I actually slept through half of one of the ones I had attended but in my defense I had been skiing all day and was pretty pooped—but "when in Rome," or in this case, when in Verona, not attending this festival would be like an international visitor coming to my part of Alberta in the beginning of July and *not* taking in at least one day of the Calgary Stampede or one of its free pancake breakfasts. Before leaving Canada, I had seen the options for that year's opera festival and *Madame Butterfly*, set in Japan, jumped out at me simply because of the time I spent living in Japan. I knew that if I was thoroughly confused or bored stiff by the plot and singing, at least I would have a great appreciation for the costumes and set.

We entered the arena on the *one day* of my entire trip thus far in which rain was in the forecast. It had sprinkled off and on during the day and the sky was threatening more. We were well aware that if it was raining, the show would be cancelled as the orchestra could not play outside and risk damaging their instruments. We knew that if the show was cancelled before Act I was finished, we would get a refund, but it wasn't much consolation because we had no other opportunity to see the show after that, our last night in the area.

When we found our seats, the clouds continued to threaten, but the show went on without a drop of rain falling. During Act I, I found myself nodding and saying to myself, *Yeah, this is the same as the other two operas I've been to and exactly what I envision opera to be. Various male and female characters standing on stage, not moving except maybe waving their arms*

Wine, Bach, and Cuckoo Clocks

dramatically now and then, singing seemingly-endless songs in a language I can't understand, and taking three minutes to say hello or how are you. And taking at least ten minutes to die. Well, I chose this one because of the costumes and set, and those are certainly colourful and impressive. And I'm glad I read the plot summary before coming because otherwise I'd have no clue what was going on.

As we left our seats to stretch our legs during intermission, a bit of rain started coming down, and all spectators huddled in the ancient hallways trying to find cover. It was getting chilly, but more than anything, we were hoping the rain would let up so that Act II could begin. For forty-five minutes, we watched the time tick by as the rain continued, and then, slowly the rain started to let up.

Yes, it stopped raining! An announcement was made in Italian, which I assumed was directing everyone back to their seats. The crowd started to move, and we made our way back to our wet chairs.

Workers cleared water off the stage with large brooms. When they were done, the orchestra members came out and settled into their seats.

I felt two drops of rain and watched as the orchestra members got up and left again. Two drops. That's all it would take to ruin one of those expensive instruments, and so we waited. A bit more rain sprinkled down, and we stayed put.

The rain stopped again, and again, workers came out to clear the water off the stage.

"The workers with brooms are getting more applause from the audience than any of the performers have so far," I said to Marina.

The orchestra came back out. They started tuning their instruments, and just as they settled back, ready to commence with Act II, the rain began again. Off they went.

It looks like we're not going to get to see Act II. Great. That means if I ever want to see Act II, I'll have to endure Act I again.

By this time, it had been an hour and forty-five minutes since the intermission had begun. Their policy was to wait up to two hours and if the show couldn't resume in two hours or less, it would be cancelled. There was still a fifteen-minute period of hope, but we were cold, tired, and disappointed, and we were sure the show was about to be cancelled. The four of us agreed that we were ready to call it a night, so we left the arena and went across the street to a café for a late-night hot chocolate.

We had been sitting at the café for a few minutes when we heard the announcement from the arena that the rest of the performance was cancelled. We sat there drinking hot chocolate, watching the crowd spill out of the arena.

***

My friends back home were again merciless when I posted pictures on Facebook of my day trip to Venice. Of course, even though it's terribly touristy, I *had* to take a trip on the Grand Canal in a gondola, and of course my gondolier was stereotypically gorgeous. It wasn't lost on me that Venice is a romantic city with its singing gondoliers, its stunning night scenes of the lights of the city reflecting off the canals, and its legend of Casanova. And there I was, travelling solo, admiring all of this—including my gondolier—thinking back to the man who had picked me up at the airport, and lamenting how I had missed my chance to have him chauffer me around the whole country. Sigh. Ah well. Some things are best left as dreams.

Venice is where I ate the best tomatoes of my life and where I bought a carnival mask to hang on my wall at home. The legend behind the mask is that it represents the flowing veil of the woman who oared Casanova away from the prison in a gondola the night he escaped—the wind blowing her veil across her face while she piloted the gondola. The true story of his escape is not nearly as romantic:

> They [Casanova and Father Balbi, a monk ... who escaped with him] escaped into the darkness, leaving behind only a note. Like something out of an adventure novel, they stole across the rooftops, prying open windows and descending bed sheet ropes on their way to freedom.[21]

I prefer the story behind my mask, which is hanging on my bedroom wall, inspiring my dreams.

***

Wine, Bach, and Cuckoo Clocks

I didn't bring any handsome Italian men home with me, but I would have dearly loved to have brought some cannoli with me.

As if my jaw wasn't sore enough after dropping nonstop over several days in Rome touring the Colosseum, The Forum, and the Spanish Steps, and after laying eyes on the Grand Canal as well St Mark's Square in Venice, Florence was where my brain finally became saturated with all the culture, and I filled my belly with more delights.

The bakery across the street from my hotel had three kinds of cannoli: chocolate, vanilla, and pistachio. I was there for four days. I decided I had to try each kind to determine which was the best, and then on my final day, have my favourite one more time. I started with pistachio.

My hotel was within walking distance of great shops and the **Accademia Gallery,** the home of Michelangelo's *David*. I had come to Florence for one reason only: to see this masterpiece that I first saw on paper when Marina sent me a postcard of the statue. I have always been fascinated and captivated by this image. No, not because of his nakedness, although as a twelve-year old, I did think it was rather scandalous that I had this postcard in my possession. (I still have it.) But I knew well the story of David and Goliath, and I valued it as a great lesson for underdogs and the "never give up" spirit.

I also knew of Michelangelo's greatness—how revered he was for his works including the Sistine Chapel. I have always been astounded at how intricately he was able to carve this statue of such a well-known Biblical character.

On my first day in Florence, I stopped in some shops, debating whether to buy a horrifically expensive leather jacket (I didn't), walked along the riverbank, and was amused at the fake statues of David that are dispersed around the city.

When I stumbled upon the first Fake David at the Palazzo Vecchio, Florence's town hall building, I was momentarily confused.

What is he doing out here in the elements? Why would they move him from inside a museum to outside, where weather and bird poop can wreak havoc on this masterpiece?

I realized I was not looking at the original and did my homework to find out that yes, this was one of several replicas in the city.

On my second day, I joined a tour. A cooking tour! I was one member of a group of eight who had signed up to learn how to cook some Italian food. Our tour began at a market, where our guide showed us different types of meats and cheeses and gave us some samples. He then bought the ingredients he needed for our cooking course, and we set off to the winery where our lesson was to take place. On our way, we stopped at a lookout over town where yet another Fake David was perched, keeping watch over Florence. Two Fake Davids—three Davids to go, including the real one.

I had a bit of an edge for the first part of our lesson: making fresh pasta. For as long as I could remember, my parents and grandparents had made fresh, homemade noodles once or twice a year, as often as needed to keep us in stock. It was a full-day event with Mom or Grandma using a dozen eggs to make a huge batch of dough, which they then put through the pasta machine to cut fettuccini noodles. We dried them on bed sheets on the floor in the living room and on clothing racks and then stored them in airtight containers.

Our instructor stepped us through making individual-sized pasta balls with one egg and the right amount of flour to mix with the egg. Our pasta on this day would not be dried; it would be cooked fresh with marinara sauce. While our baseball-sized balls of dough were resting, our instructor put us to work cutting tomatoes, garlic, onion, and fresh herbs to help make the massive batch of marinara sauce. And then, while that was cooking, we made our dessert: tiramisu.

I love this dessert—the lightness of it, the flavours, the textures. I guess it was an attempt to be authentic and ensure maximum lightness, but our instructor made us beat the egg whites by hand. When was the last time anyone on this planet has done this? I was sure that even the best Italian mothers use electric eggbeaters, but that wasn't an option for us. We had to switch off several times, taking turns beating them, as each person only had a few minutes before our arms were sore.

At last, the egg whites were stiff and we were able to make our individual cups of tiramisu. We started by placing the ladyfingers in the cups and then layering the rest of the ingredients. Each person decorated the top of their cup differently so we would know whose was whose after the desserts were chilled, and we could eat our own.

We placed our cups on a baking sheet and our instructor took them to the refrigerator in the back to chill.

CRAAAASH.

We looked at each other.

"That doesn't bode well for our tiramisu," I said to the rest of the group, worried that we had just forfeited our dessert.

Our instructor returned moments later, a sheepish look all over his face.

"When I was putting the tray into the fridge, I bumped it and several of your desserts were knocked to the ground."

Ugh. I had been looking forward to dessert.

"So some of your desserts were destroyed, but we have some extras in the fridge, so everyone will get one even though some of you may not get your own."

Our group happily finished preparations for our dinner. We ooh-ed and aah-ed over the local pre-dinner wine we were drinking while the pasta cooked, and when it was ready, we sat down for our meal. There is no comparison to homemade pasta versus dried, store-bought pasta, no matter how good the pre-packaged pasta is. We mmm-ed and yum-ed our way through the meal and then looked forward to dessert.

My tiramisu was one of the ones that had taken a dive, so I ate one of the extra ones that had already been in the fridge. No matter. I've never met a tiramisu I didn't get along with, and I took comfort in knowing that they all tasted the same anyway since we all took our ingredients from the same bowls.

After filling our bellies, we got in the van and went back to town. Our guide dropped us each off at our hotels, and before entering my hotel, I zipped across the street to the bakery.

This day was chocolate cannoli day. Good—but not quite as good as the pistachio.

***

On my third day, I joined a walking tour of the area near my hotel that included stops in some of the local museums, including the Accademia Gallery. I wanted a guided tour to talk me through the truckloads of art history in this city, including my long-lost friend

In Search of David

David. I love to explore on my own, but the information a great tour guide can provide is priceless, so I shook my head, cleared some space in my brain for some art history—a topic I know almost nothing about—and donned my walking shoes.

Speaking of walking shoes, this was Italy. So … good shoes, good leather, good fashion. When I was staying in Abana Terme, I wandered the town a bit to explore. It's not a big town, but it's easy to get around.

After years of travelling and bringing back kitschy souvenirs that meet their end in a garage sale, a box, or the garbage, I have stopped bringing much back when I travel. I limit myself to items that are edible and one or two extravagant nice souvenirs for myself. I had the mask from Venice, but that was going on the wall. It wasn't something I could use on a daily basis other than to look at it and appreciate the artistry of it. I was on a mission for shoes.

Abana Terme had several shoe shops, all within two blocks of each other. I looked in each of them and narrowed down my choice to one store that had a few pairs in navy blue (blue is one of my favourite colours) patent leather (I love patent leather shoes). I was drawn to one pair, but I loved the price of another pair better. I pondered the two options, trying one on, then the other, back and forth.

Finally I said, "Screw it. I'm in Italy, and this is a nice purchase for myself. Something I can use a lot."

I bought the more expensive pair. Shiny patent leather Oxford style slip-on shoes with sparkly grey-blue fabric as a contrast. Years later, I still get compliments whenever I wear them and I tell the other party, "I paid far too much, but I bought them in Italy. I'm not a shoe girl but I love them." The most common reply I get from women is, "There's no such thing as paying too much for a great pair of shoes."

Back to Florence. Our tour guide predictably gave us a great deal of information about art history and how to properly observe art. He pointed out that Renaissance painters wanted to ensure that those viewing their paintings got a great perspective regardless of the angle from which they were viewing. I tried his suggestion of looking at certain parts of certain paintings from different angles and sure enough, the 3D perspective showed itself from any angle. Fascinating and impressive.

He toured us around the Uffizi Gallery, inside and out, explaining who the statues were commemorating and what their contributions to the Florence art scene were. The gallery contains paintings, busts, and sculptures created by 14th-century and Renaissance artists such as Giotto, Botticelli, Michelangelo, and many more. And then we went to the Accademia Gallery, which he had saved for last.

He gave us a brief introduction to the museum in the entrance and toured us through the first sections, pointing out the different pieces and who had created them. Before we got to the statue of *David*, he pulled us together and told us that it was considered a masterpiece because Michelangelo had exacted the dimensions and created such fine detail in correct proportions. He told us that before we got to the chamber that contained *David*, we would see this and that, and then he set us free to move forward through the museum.

I started out, looking at the different smaller statues to my left and right as I progressed, preparing myself for the moment when I would finally see what I had come to Florence to see. As I passed the last of the statues on my left and right and stepped into the next room, I gasped. There he was.

I stood with my mouth open, admiring the statue to my right. I had known since childhood what this statue looked like but to see the gleaming white marble, the tall figure of this significant character from Biblical stories, in the natural sunlight beaming down from the windows in the dome above it, was not something I was prepared for. On one hand, it's just a statue, but on the other, it *is* a masterpiece. Some things are not worth the hype. *David* is.

I moved toward it, surprised that it was not encased in glass or any other protective covering. All that separated the statue from the throngs of people was a rope barrier. Some damage is visible from up close. Apparently not even this statue is immune to vandalism, but in spite of the fact that it has been damaged, curators keep it accessible to the public, many of whom are respectful, but of course there were the titters and giggles and people who were taking closeups of the genitalia.

Interestingly, the back of the statue is quite plain. I took a picture zooming in on his bum rather than on what is in front, because we rarely see the backside of *David*.

In Search of David

At the end of the tour, I made my way back to my hotel, stopping for the daily cannoli, this time vanilla. After I got into bed, I tried to wrap my head around all the incredible history and art I had seen in the previous twelve days. I needed to recharge all of my senses.

And I needed to vote. It was not a competition. The pistachio cannoli won hands down, so the next day, before I left Florence to head back to Rome, I stopped at the bakery one more time for a pistachio cannoli and ate it while giving a "cheers" to the city that had overwhelmed my senses for three days.

***

After resolving the cannoli dilemma and visiting The Very Famous and Revered Statue, I took the train back to Rome. I had one more box to check off my list before having a final dinner with Marina and then heading to Germany: The Vatican.

I had saved it for the end because I figured since it was technically an entirely different country, I should "do" Italy first.

I had signed up for a VIP tour, so I got to see the behind-the-scenes buildings and gardens that are only accessible to visitors on such a tour. Alas, there were no sightings of the Pope himself, nor did I catch a glimpse of any members of the Swiss Guard. The gardens, though, were lush, colourful, and well-kept, and the trickling of the fountains was relaxing.

Of course the highlight was a visit to Michelangelo's other masterpiece (Ok, I know he has a few …), the Sistine Chapel, or, as my sister and I irreverently call it, The Sixteenth Chapel.

Years earlier when Janice was touring Italy, she posted pictures on Facebook of the sights she was seeing. At one point, I commented, "When are you going to see The Sixteenth Chapel? And have you seen the first fifteen yet?"

Someone who didn't even know me and who didn't get my humour "corrected" me: "It's the Sistine Chapel." Ahhhh social media, where people who don't even know each other feel the need to butt into conversations that don't involve them and show they know more than people they have never met.

But she played right along.

Wine, Bach, and Cuckoo Clocks

"The other fifteen aren't worth going to," she replied.

After seeing it with my own eyes, I would be inclined to agree.

I was surprised at how small the Sistine Chapel is. It was probably good for Michelangelo's back and shoulders that the Chapel isn't the size of the massive European cathedrals I expected it to match. The grandeur is in the detail of the paintings and the skill it took to create them. There wasn't a time limit on how long I could stay in the Chapel, gazing at the ceiling. The only rule was "no photography," and several times I heard security guards approach tourists who ignored the rule and bark at them, "No photo!"

I could have spent hours there, studying each scene, replaying the stories from the Bible that they represented, looking at all of the details. Eventually, though, my eyes started to glaze over, and my brain and retinas reached their saturation point.

The tour path continues through the Chapel to the adjoining St. Peter's Basilica, which I also spent a bit of time in, again, looking at the marble and the architectural design. Until I entered them, I wasn't aware that St. Peter's holds the tombs of previous popes. With my fascination for the morbid combined with my respect for history and religious significance, I walked past several of the tombs, observing the names and in some cases, the mummified bodies of previous popes.

I'd heard of St. Peter's Basilica my whole life, and I knew it as the church where the Pope speaks to people from time to time. But I didn't know much about it beyond that.

Of course it makes sense that St. Peter's holds the tombs of former popes, just as other churches in Europe contain the tombs of other famous citizens: Bach's remains in St. Thomas Church in Leipzig, Shakespeare in the Holy Trinity Church in Stratford-Upon-Avon, Martin Luther in the Castle Church in Wittenburg, and among many more, pretty much every king and queen in European history.

I'd also forgotten how the construction of the Basilica was funded (I'd learned this in school as a kid but was reminded of it at St. Peter's):

> One method employed to finance the building of St. Peter's Basilica was the granting of indulgences [payments made to the Catholic Church in the Middle Ages in exchange for being absolved of one's sins] in return for contributions. ... A German Augustinian

priest, Martin Luther, wrote to Archbishop Albrecht arguing against this 'selling of indulgences.' He also included his 'Disputation of Martin Luther on the Power and Efficacy of Indulgences,' which came to be known as The Ninety-Five Theses. This became a factor in starting the Reformation, the birth of Protestantism.[22]

Ah, Luther again. I can't escape this guy, even in Italy.

***

After touring the Basilica, I exited the front doors to St. Peter's Square. The square wasn't busy; there was an averaged-sized crowd or even smaller. As I stood in the square, though, I looked around and, as I had done in Zeppelinfeld, Ghetto Hero's Square, the Colosseum, the Forum, and other historically significant places I have been, I let my imagination take hold. I looked back at the Basilica, and I could feel and imagine the excitement and significance for those who gather in this square when the Pope is giving a message.

Admittedly, it is completely irreverent to lump the Pope (any of them) into the same category as Hitler, but the common theme is that of a group gathering for a common purpose: to hear an influential leader. I thought back to concerts I've been to, and how the crowd gets swept away with emotion at being in the presence of their favourite singers or bands. I thought of video images I've seen of Queen Elizabeth and other members of the royal family standing on the balcony at Buckingham Palace, presenting themselves to the adoring crowd. Current political rallies. Girls fainting at Elvis's hip gyrations during his concerts. Today's youth screaming for Taylor Swift.

I was struck with the idea that as humans, we all have our passions: music, religion, politics. And we all need heroes. People to look up to. People who, just because of their job, we look to for guidance, inspiration, knowledge.

***

Wine, Bach, and Cuckoo Clocks

After dinner near the Vatican with Marina, Laura (her sister) and Laura's husband, I boarded my one-hour flight to Germany and started turning myself off of tourist mode. When Christine picked me up at the other side of that hour, I gave her a hug and told her, "I have no emotions left. Italy is just too much for us stoic Germans."

Martin Luther's Fifteen Minutes

By 2023 and after visiting Germany several times, I wanted to delve more deeply into Martin Luther's story. My tour of Torgau brought me to his world, but I hadn't yet been to Erfurt or Wittenburg, two of the main cities that are associated with Luther. I felt that I needed to fill this knowledge gap for myself.

At home in Canada, I did some research to see if I could find Luther-themed tours of Germany or certain towns and cities where Luther had worked and preached. There were a few, mostly geared toward church groups coming as a group. I also found a gentleman who would customize a private tour for me of "Luther-land" for five days, ending in Leipzig. His itinerary sounded thorough and interesting.

But I thought, *I don't need to do such extensive, intensive Luther-related travel. Five days is a lot of time spent talking about one guy.*

I decided to try and include a day in each of Erfurt and Wittenberg next time I was in Germany.

Every October, my mom's cousins get together for lunch in central Alberta. The get-together started as a gathering several years ago for a few of them to make sure they connected in person once a year, and over time, it's morphed into an "anyone who can make it" afternoon. I'd never attended until after my mom had died. After her death, I took my dad to the Cousin's Lunch feeling like the time spent with my mom's side of the family would be good for us both.

I've attended a few times, but there have also been a couple of times that I intended to go but couldn't because of bad driving conditions or health problems. I was sick in October 2023 and couldn't make the trip to the lunch. That evening, a number of attendees commented in the group chat in Messenger how nice it was to see everyone and that they were already looking forward to next year.

"Same time same place next year if everyone's Ok with that," my uncle confirmed.

"I think next year's lunch should be in the Bahamas," I replied. I couldn't suppress my smartassed nature.

"Or Germany," my mom's cousin Marietta replied.

"Germany would be great!" another cousin said.

A few others added their thanks to my uncle for organizing the event and the chat quieted down for the night.

The next day, I messaged Marietta privately.

"Did we inadvertently sign ourselves up for organizing next year's lunch?" I asked her. "I don't know about you, but I was just being a smartass and joking about going to the Bahamas, but I got the sense that some people were open to the idea of a group of us going to Germany."

"There's a family reunion every year near the end of September in Germany," she replied. "I went to it last year, and I plan on going next year. You should come too. I think you'd enjoy it."

"That does sound like fun! Let me know the details, and I'll think about it."

She sent me the email address of Heidrun, the woman in Germany who organizes the annual reunion and sends out a newsletter every month or two to members of the reunion group.

"Tell her you are my grandpa's great granddaughter. She'll know how you fit into the family and will add you to the mailing list for the newsletter and send you information about the reunion when they know the dates and location. It's in a different town each year."

I emailed Heidrun, who replied with a warm email thanking me for getting in touch and telling me how much she would love to meet me if I could come to the reunion in September 2024. She also sent me a friend request on Facebook.

Eleven months later, Marietta, her husband (Eric), another extended family member from Alberta (Karen), whom I hadn't met until that morning at the airport, and I boarded a plane in Calgary and flew to Germany together.

The four of us wanted to go to Wittenberg since none of us had been there and it is brimming with museums (I was ready for an hour in a Luther-related museum but no more than that), churches, and other sites that played a significant role in the Reformation. We were disappointed to learn upon our arrival that Lutherhaus, Martin Luther's home in Wittenberg, was closed for the next two years for renovations, but there was no lack of other sites to visit.

We began our self-guided tour at Augusteum, featuring "Literally Luther," an exhibition of artifacts, paintings, and other items organized alphabetically outlining Luther's life, studies, and work. The exhibit was interesting and informative but what entertained me the most was the woman working inside the exhibition rooms. She had a knack for appearing suddenly, without warning, and from seemingly nowhere with an intimidating presence. Karen was using walking sticks to help support her back and dropped one while looking at one of the exhibits. The clattering of the stick hitting the floor echoed loudly throughout the room. Instantly, the woman working there appeared beside us (from where? I had no idea she was even around), snatched the stick, took the other one from Karen's hand, and told her, "I will take these to the first floor. You can get them there when you are finished."

Karen and I exchanged glances of bemusement. We were not only startled at the woman's sudden and brusque appearance but unsure of whether to laugh or be offended at her assertiveness.

The woman continued to randomly pop up as I made my way through the exhibit, giving me a glance now and then. I felt like I was being scrutinized by an undercover police detective and had to suppress my giggles.

Maybe she thinks I'm hiding an expandable baseball bat in my pocket, and I'm going to take it out and start smashing the whole exhibit or something. Why doesn't she trust us?

I almost lost my composure when I was playing with an exhibit that consisted of five keys hanging on pegs; there were three holes above the keys, and the goal was to find which three keys opened the display, revealing the final piece of information about the display. I had just inserted the last correct key and turned it, prompting the light to go on, when the woman again popped up beside me and said, "That is for children!" I pulled the keys out and walked away, covering my mouth with my hand and trying my damnedest not to burst out laughing.

This is why some people stereotype German people as being harsh and rude. I knew she was just doing her job, but her demeanour came off as rough and intimidating.

But I found her behaviour to be hilarious, especially the fact that she continuously and suddenly popped up regardless of which room I was in, as if she were a plastic rodent in a combination of a maze and a live game of whac-a-mole.

From that building, we then moved on to tour the Melanchthonhaus.

"Melanchthon. Who is he?" Karen asked.

"He was one of Luther's cohorts. Cronies? I don't know what the best word is. I guess we'll find out more once we tour his house. What I do know is that Luther gets so much of the credit for the Reformation, but there was a group of them who worked together pushing for change. Luther is the most famous of them because he nailed The Ninety-Five Theses to the door of the church, but several of them worked together to challenge the Catholic Church," I replied.

Melanchthon, as an influential scholar during the period of the Reformation, came up with several new religious motifs and "advised the artists on theological questions. Together they developed picture panels on the Biblical commandments, thus enabling a broad section of the population to access the new understanding of faith."[23]

Melanchthonhaus is a building showcasing excellent information about Philipp Melanchthon's life, family, and work as a professor. After touring the building, we had a much deeper understanding of who he was and why his work is celebrated.

From there, we walked to the Castle Church.

The main attraction on the outside of the church is the location of the door where Luther nailed his Ninety-Five Theses. The actual wooden door was destroyed in a fire in 1760 during the Seven Years' War, but in its place now is a bronze door on which Luther's Ninety-Five Theses have been etched in Latin.

The bronze door isn't functional, so to enter the church, visitors must go around to the other side of the building and enter via the visitor's entrance. The church is to the right of the visitor entrance and hosts some of the most detailed and captivating stained glass I have ever seen: images portraying the crucifixion and resurrection of Christ as well as the main figures of the Reformation. As I sat on the front pew, behind the tombs of both Luther and Melanchthon, I concluded that one could sit there for hours, examining the detail of the stained glass and still miss a great many details.

I was the only one in the church for several minutes, so I was able to take a few moments of silence and think about the huge impact these two men, and others, had on world and religious history because of their actions centuries ago. I thought of my great-grandpa and his ancestors being Lutheran, and I reviewed the puzzle pieces I have put together throughout my life of family connections to Germany through food, religion, and personal relationships. I felt like the puzzle was nearly complete. My Lutheran ancestors were in this land until religious persecution drove them out. They settled in Russia, which was offering them freedom of language, religion, and culture. And freedom from paying taxes. But when new Russian rulers came along and revoked those privileges, my ancestors migrated again, some to North and South America, others back to Germany, seeking a better life.

I tallied my freedoms: freedom to practice a religion or not and if so, freedom to choose which one; freedom of speech; freedom to vote (or not, if I choose) in my country's elections; freedom to choose my career, and so much more. Compared to my ancestors, and to those like Christine who grew up in communist countries, I've had a pretty easy life that is rich with opportunity and choice.

I also reflected on additional work that Luther and these other men did that have a direct impact on my daily life—the fact that I love to read, the fact that I write and make my living by using written communication.

The invention of the printing press allowed people like Luther to spread their ideas more quickly and easily to the general population. Luther's Ninety-Five Theses were not the only history-changing actions he took. His translation of the Bible into German and the ability, with the invention of the printing press, for the Bible to then be printed and distributed to the masses turned Christianity upside down. One of my friends often says, "Sometimes two things can happen at once." What he means is, two simultaneous and otherwise unconnected events can tie together to create a result that no one saw coming. Thus was the case with Luther:

Church doors were a bit like local bulletin boards, for priests, circulating news and information such as the announcement of a lost kitten or objections to the supreme authority of the Catholic Church. Martin Luther's Ninety-Five Theses was a first draft of his complaints, submitted to a close circle of academics. 'My purpose was not to publish them,' he wrote to one printer. 'Thus I [thought to] either destroy them if condemned or edit them with the approbation of others. But now that they are printed and circulated far beyond my expectation, I feel anxious about what they may bring forth.'

Feeling anxious was right. The insatiable machinations of the printing press were about to spread Martin Luther's words throughout all of Europe and launch a religious revolution in his name. Luther himself thought the presses a difficult beast to control. 'This method is not the best adapted to instruct the public,' he mused. 'I should have spoken far differently and more distinctly had I known what was going to happen.'

...

Once Luther learned to embrace the printing press, his ideas spread farther and faster than he ever imagined .... Some historians believe the true beginning of the Reformation happened at the moment Luther started printing in the common German tongue. His campaign enabled the average citizen to read (or at least hear) arguments about religion in a way he or she could easily understand.[24]

While visiting the small museum that is joined to the Castle Church, I read Luther's Ninety-Five Theses for the first time. Reading all of them didn't enlighten me to much I didn't already know; they were boring and wordy with lots of "therefores," and "yeas," and "doths," and "wherebys." I had, in my childhood learnings, gotten the gist of who Luther was and the impact he had on Christianity as well as bringing the Bible to everyday people by having it printed in

German. I've always been grateful for the Christian teachings I received as a child as they set the foundation for the values and principles I try to live by. I've probably also always had a bit more respect for Luther because, as someone who challenges the status quo if I see the potential to do something in a better way, I can identify with the frustration he must have felt with the Catholic Church, and I respect people who rebel against authority in the name of progress.

Cousins by the Dozen

"Family comes first."

I can't count how many times I heard my grandma say this during the forty years she was in my life. Many members of my family place a strong emphasis on family, but Grandma lived her philosophy to the fullest. It was because of her that I knew my great-grandpa as well as I did. I often wonder if I would have felt a similarly strong connection to any of my other great-grandparents had they been alive when I was growing up. I never had the chance to know them, and I haven't had the same intrigue about them as I have always had about Great-Grandpa, perhaps simply because I had the opportunity to know him, and I have memories of interacting with him.

Grandma also put a great emphasis on keeping in touch with her sisters and brother, so when my cousin Marietta, daughter of one of my grandma's sisters, suggested I join her and her husband in Germany for the family reunion, I was excited for a number of reasons, one of which was to be able to spend more time with her; we live about four hours from each other so we don't get to see each other often. The fact that Marietta had attended the Germany family reunion two years prior and would know many of the attendees made my decision easier; I wanted to go and meet these extended family members, and she could help me bridge the distance.

Each year, the reunion is held wherever the person helping organize it lives. The family reunion for 2024 was in Hankensbüttel, a town of fewer than 5,000 people near Hamburg and Hannover. Marietta, Eric, Karen, and I arrived on the Friday afternoon, the day before the official reunion began. Several other family members were arriving Friday from various parts of Germany, so dinner reservations had been made for ten of us at a local Greek restaurant. The program for the reunion didn't begin until Saturday afternoon, with cake and coffee, but as we were finishing our meal Friday night, Ulrich, the family member who lived in Hankensbüttel and who was organizing much of the reunion, said that he would take anyone who was interested on a nature walk starting at ten the next morning. I indicated that I was interested, and we all said goodnight to each other. Ulrich and his family went home and the rest of us went to the local guest house, where we were staying and where the formal reunion schedule would take place.

The walking path Ulrich took us on was a ten-minute drive outside of town. I loved the fall colours on the nature walk on this warm, sunny autumn day. Much of the grass was still green, but a lot of the natural brush was yellow, tan, and bronze. Fields of heather were at the end of blooming, and the odd purple flower stalk was still visible among the drying foliage, giving the fields a light lavender hue. We walked for three kilometres, doing a loop from the parking lot, where a little pay-what-you-will stand filled with pumpkins and five different kinds of squash was located. We returned to the guest house to find that more family members had arrived and were sitting on the patio.

One of the new arrivals was a man I had been looking forward to meeting for several months. A few days after Heidrun had welcomed me to the family Facebook group, Peter posted photos of two documents showing that in the 1700s, a woman whose last name was Stuber had married one of the ancestors on this, my mother's side of the family. Of course this piqued my curiosity, and I was anxious to meet Peter and ask him more about what he knew of this woman.

He and three others were sitting and having a beer. They stood up when we approached the entrance to the guest house, and we shook hands with all four of them.

"Peter," he introduced himself.

"Hallo, Lorna," I replied.

"Lorna Stuber," Peter said and started laughing.

"Ja!" I laughed as well. "Do you speak English?" I asked him.

"No!" he quickly replied and laughed again.

Dang it. I like this man already. He seems fun and good-natured. But if he doesn't speak English, I can't have an in-depth conversation about this Stuber connection and see what he knows.

Later that day, he showed me the documents he had posted pictures of, and we had a brief conversation with Marietta translating. I vowed to Peter and to myself that I'd look into this on my end and see what I could find out about my father's family being possibly connected to my mother's family as far back as 300 years ago.

After the kickoff of the reunion—coffee and cake Saturday afternoon—Heidrun presented a slide show outlining how each attendee fit into the family tree. When she introduced each person, she had us stand beside the screen showing the slide of our lineage. This was a great way for us to see who was who and how each person fit into the family. I took photos of all slides so I could remember everyone later.

Halfway through the slideshow, I turned my head from the screen to look at Marietta, my eyes bugged out.

Ernst, the man whose slide had come up, had the same last name as my grandpa. Here I was at a family reunion for my *grandma's* extended family, and a man with her married name was standing fifteen feet away.

"I wonder if I'm related to him through my grandpa, too!" I whispered to Marietta.

"Could be," she said. "You'll have to talk to him."

"I'm starting to get scared that I'm related to myself three ways!" I joked with her.

"'I Am My Own Grandpa'," she replied, citing the name of a country music song that is both hilarious and utterly confusing in outlining how the singer, because of marriage, step-children, in-laws, etc. is his own grandpa if you look at the family tree a certain way.

"This may be just my imagination, but I think he looks like my grandpa—the top half of his face," I said to Marietta.

"He has your grandpa's eyes," she replied.

Later that evening when I had a chance, my conversation with Ernst started out the same as the one with Peter.

"Do you speak English?"

"No."

But Marietta translated for us and told Ernst why I had a particular interest in learning more about him. He turned to a page in the book he was carrying and showed me the names of his grandpa, who may or may not be related to my grandpa. To my homework that I owed Peter, I added a mental note to check into my grandpa's ancestry to see if/how Ernst was related to my mom's paternal side. (When I returned home, I looked at my documents and asked some family members; our best guess is that Ernst's grandfather could have been my great-grandfather's cousin, but that's pure speculation.)

Heidrun had organized a speed-dating type activity that would allow attendees to get to know another family member better. She listed off several people and asked them to stay in their seats. The rest of us were to approach her and get a card. Each card had a different name on it—the name of one of the people who was to remain seated—and we were then to sit with the person whose name was on our card and chat for twenty minutes.

Oh no. With my limited German, this could be twenty minutes of torture for me, the other person, or both!

I momentarily contemplated escaping to the bathroom for twenty minutes.

Come on, Stuber. You may get the name of someone who speaks English well, and if not, it's a good chance for you to practice your German. After all, this is why you came to the reunion—to connect with these people you are related to.

A huge grin broke out on my face when I read the name on the card Heidrun had given me and, and as I sought out that person, I thought, *Perfect! Language won't be a problem, and I want to get to know this person better anyway!*

I plopped myself on the chair beside Ulrich.

"Does this mean I have to speak English?" he said as he laughed.

"Yes, my German is terrible!" We shared another laugh.

Ulrich was short and slight, around five-foot-seven, and probably 140 pounds at most. He had grey-blue eyes, a fabulous and meticulous white handlebar moustache, and a terrific sense of humour; like me, he seemed to be laughing more than not throughout the weekend. Once I learned he had been a police officer, I begin to imagine him as a black-capped policeman in a Steve Martin comedy movie, pencil poised above notepad, ready to write out a traffic ticket: "Und vye ah you pah-ked hee-ah? Ziss iss a no pah-king zone!" His character's name would have been Herr Inspektor.

"Thank you again for organizing the walk this morning. It was a beautiful day, and the walking path was lovely. I really enjoyed it. Have you lived here all your life?" I said.

"Yes, with my wife, and now my ninety-one-year-old mother lives with us." He pointed to the woman sitting across the table from us who was looking across the room at a group of other people. She looked more like seventy-one than ninety-one.

"Oh how wonderful! And are you retired?"

"Yes. I was a policeman, but now I'm retired."

"Interesting. But I'm sure in a small town like this you didn't have to solve murders or much other serious crime."

"No, there were murders! All kinds of crime. Here and in other nearby towns."

Despite a few minor gaps in his English vocabulary, our conversation flowed freely and easily. We covered various topics including food.

"You know Strudel?" he asked me. "Not the dessert, the dumpling type of Strudel."

"Yes, I love Strudel!"

"My mother taught me how to make Strudel. She told me I have to pull the dough so thin that when you hold it up, you can read a newspaper through it."

"That's exactly what my grandma used to say! That must be part of the family recipe!"

"Yes, it must be."

When I was growing up, we never had the sweet kind of Strudels—the dessert pastries found in bakeries; if Mom made something like that, they were just "turnovers." Our Strudels were made from dough that is stretched thin, rolled up until the roll is one inch thick, and then cut into three-inch rolls. Mom steamed them on top of chicken or beef stew, and it was required that the Strudels be topped with Roger's Golden Syrup. To eat them without the syrup was just not acceptable, nor was eating them with any other syrup.

I was astounded that here, thousands of miles away from where I had grown up eating my mom's and grandma's Strudels, I was sitting beside a man whose mother used the exact words my grandma used when explaining how to make a family favourite. I didn't ask Ulrich if a certain type of syrup was required in his household.

***

Another of Ulrich's other main contributions to the reunion was a friendly competition on the Saturday evening: a Bessarabian quiz. He asked us to organize ourselves into teams of three or four and then presented a quiz of eighteen questions. The other three Canadians were sticking together, and Anke, one of our cousins from Berlin, was sitting on the other side of them from where I was, so I teamed up with Ulrich's wife, sister, and our ringer: his ninety-one-year-old mother.

"I guess I'm the team's handicap," I said as I shuffled my chair closer to Mama.

Ulrich's quiz was a PowerPoint presentation with one slide for each question, the questions in both German and English. Several questions were along the lines of, "The Bessarabian word ____ means _____." Others were about Bessarabian farm tools or foods, and all questions were multiple choice, with four possible answers.

I had no clue what the answers to any of them were. Mama seemed confident in about half or more of her answers, but she didn't seem to grasp the concept of this being a competition. As Ulrich presented the questions and the answer choices, Mama nodded or shook her head at each answer choice or responded audibly, telling her daughter loud enough for the rest of the room to hear, what the correct answer was.

"Mama!" Ulrich's sister repeatedly scolded her along with a great deal of laughter.

My fellow Canadians, along with Anke, were the winners of the quiz. The rest of us applauded their victory.

Food: The Universal Language

My immediate family and my grandparents on both sides ate a lot of dough when I was growing up. My favourite type of fresh pasta was what we called "nefflies."

Neffla, nefflies, or Gniftale, as I've seen it called in some old cookbooks, is basically our version of gnocchi. The closest real German word for the form of dough I have found is Schupfnudel:

> Schupfnudel (German; plural Schupfnudeln), also called Fingernudel (finger noodle), is a type of dumpling or thick noodle in southern German and Austrian cuisine. It is similar to the Central European kopytka and Italian gnocchi. They take various forms and can be referred to with a variety of names in different regions. They are usually made from rye or wheat flour and egg. Since the introduction of the potato to Germany in the seventeenth century, Schupfnudeln have also been made with potatoes. They are traditionally given their distinctive ovoid shape through hand-shaping and are often served as a savoury dish with sauerkraut but are also served in sweet dishes.[25]

We made nefflies from the same ingredients as any type of standard pasta: egg, flour, salt. Unlike Strudel, when it came time to roll out the dough for nefflies, the goal was not to get it as thin as possible as it was for the Strudels. Mom and my grandmas instead aimed for a thickness of half an inch. Once the dough was rolled out, they cut it into strips of half an inch wide. Then, they held each strip over a pot of boiling water while snipping pieces of the dough off, one inch long or less, dropping the "dough boys," as we also called them, into the boiling water. The pieces of dough weren't the oblong shape of a finger that show up in pictures found in a Google search for Schupfnudel; they were similar size and shape to gnocchi.

Once they were cooked through, Mom or my grandmas fried the nefflies in butter until they were crispy.

Until I was an adult, I had never heard the word gnocchi. We called these little bites of dough rubber notchies in addition to nefflies. I had always thought the term rubber notchies was a slam against them because they were more dense than regular noodles and could sometimes get a bit chewy. But as an adult, I wonder if notchies may be a bastardization of gnocchi.

Saturday morning of the reunion, at breakfast, I was listening to the conversation and trying to understand as much as possible. I was sitting across the table from Gerhard, one of the pleasant older gentlemen who had a booming voice and a gregarious presence.

Suddenly I caught one word in Gerhard's speaking that made me sit up and pay close attention to the conversation.

"Bla bla Knöpfle bla bla." (Knöpfle is pronounced kə-nəp-fleh)

Knöpfle? As in ... nefflies? Until this moment, I've never heard anyone outside of my family use this word! But then Gerhard is family. How interesting that my family in Canada uses this word and now a family member in Germany has used it as well. I've never heard anyone else in Germany ever use this word, and I've tried numerous times to search how to spell it, but I've found nothing.

I focused in on his conversation with the person beside him.

"Bla bla bla Knöpfle bla bla Spätzle bla bla bla Knöpfle."

From the words I recognized and the body language and hand gestures, I could discern that these two men were having a heavy-duty discussion about various types of dough in German cuisine. Still I was puzzled. I'd had Spätzle many times in Germany and in German restaurants elsewhere, but my mother and grandmas almost never made Spätzle. They made Knöpfle often though, and my grandma's Knöpfle soup—a homemade chicken noodle soup with chunks of carrots and potatoes and Knöpfle as the noodles—was always a favourite in the winter or when I wanted comfort food when I was living three hours from home attending university.

"Bla bla bla Knöpfle Suppe bla bla bla," Gerhard continued.

Knöpfle soup?! Now I'm craving my grandma's Knöpfle soup.

I wished I could understand more of and take part in this conversation. My limited vocabulary prohibited me from doing so in German, and I didn't want to interrupt the conversation in English, so I continued to listen.

Food: The Universal Language

After breakfast, when Marietta and I were walking up the stairs to our guest rooms, she asked me, "Did you get much of that discussion about dough?"

"Not really but it sounded like it was quite a heated debate." I laughed.

"Yeah, they were arguing over which type of noodle was better, Knöpfle or Spätzle."

"Ha! That's so funny since they are pretty much the same thing, aren't they? Just a different shape and size? I'll happily take either any day of the week."

***

By this time, at age fifty-five, I had finally formed an understanding that while some foods in Germany are universal (sauerkraut, potato salad, pork everything), each region has its own take on those common dishes as well as their own dishes. Over the years since I started travelling to Germany, I also began to learn about Schwabian culture, including Schwabian food.

> Schwabians ... are a Germanic-speaking people who are native to the ethnocultural and linguistic region of Schwabia, which is now mostly divided between the modern states of Baden-Württemberg and Bavaria, in southwestern Germany.[26]

Germany, Prussia, Russia, Romania, Bessarabia, Moldova, Schwabia, Saxony ... Canada! What exactly am I?

This question brings to mind a question my students often asked me when I was teaching in Japan: "What is a typical Canadian food?"

I always had a hard time answering this question. The answer was a long and complicated one:

"Well, it depends on where you live, where you grew up, and what your ancestry is. On the west coast, salmon is one of the most common foods because a lot of salmon fishing is done in the west. And if you live on the east coast, lobster is more common than it is anywhere else in Canada. If you live in my area, in Alberta, one of the main industries is beef, so a lot of people in Alberta would say a hamburger or steak is

Wine, Bach, and Cuckoo Clocks

a typical food for them, but my family ate a lot of German food when I was growing up because of the types of cooking passed down through my ancestors, and we also had a lot of pork and chicken, because we grew all those animals on our farm. A Canadian who has Italian ancestry probably eats a lot of pasta. There's no such thing as a typical Canadian food because Canadians are so diverse."

I'm starting to understand that even within my family, which, to my knowledge, has no other European influence, "German" doesn't suffice to describe my ancestry. The migration of my direct ancestors from Germany to Bessarabia and then to Canada meant that German influence came along with them, but along the way, other Eastern European influence crept in. Thus our inclusion of cabbage rolls, perogies, and other Eastern European foods on our dinner tables.

Even with German being my foundational culture, I've come to understand that "German" is a much broader term than I had ever realized. My family's food and German dialect seem to be rooted in Schwabian Germany, so I have more in common with people from that area than I do with my friends in Leipzig, for example. Yet the influence of the years my ancestors spent in what is now Ukraine means that my family's culture includes more than Schwabian food.

One's cultural heritage also includes language. I studied German for two years in high school and quickly realized that the German I was learning was different from what we used (albeit sparsely) at home. When I was a kid, Mom told me that both she and Dad knew only German when they started school as five-year olds. Apparently my dad ran away from school at noon on the first day and returned home because he didn't understand what was going on and he didn't want to be there.

I had a similar experience when I started kindergarten as I didn't know the English word for flyswatter, sausage, and a few other items. When I used "our" words in school, my friends always asked, "What are you talking about?" To me, a flyswatter was a "Mookabutcha" ("butch" pronounced to rhyme with "such" and "much"). "Butch" meant "slap" or "smack" and was an onomatopoeic word Mom and Grandma used to refer to the sound created when they were smacking bread dough.

Likewise, "vorks" (with the r rolled) meant to throw up and was also therefore onomatopoeic. Sausages were "Wurst," which we pronounced "vushed" (to rhyme with "bushed"), and "vushlies" were small sausages, such as breakfast sausages or the type Mom and I ate in Nuremberg.

We pronounced "Kuchen" as "kooka," and my dad took things one step further; he had a habit of making nicknames out of words such as calling our neighbour Murray "Murphy" and talking about the "Boy Sprouts" coming to the door to sell popcorn. When he was talking about Kuchen (kooka), he called it "kookoo."

I've always known these words, or at least our pronunciation of them, were not standard German words; once I started studying German in high school, I began to suspect that they were slang words or part of a dialect that my family spoke, but I could never find any information about these words until the Internet came along. Through Internet searches and conversations with other extended family members, I learned that many of the words my family used come from a Schwabian dialect, have morphed over the years thus bastardizing the language (as my dad's pronunciation of "kuchen" did), and/or come from Ukrainian. Since my ancestors lived for several generations in what is now Ukraine, just as perogies entered our mealtimes, some Ukrainian vernacular would have entered their verbal communication.

By the end of the Saturday night of the reunion weekend, a previously missing piece of my identity clicked into place in my brain. My ancestors were not strictly German, nor were they only Schwabian. They were also Bessarabian. I am Canadian, but I'm also the other three, and that makes me part of a specific group of people: someone whose ancestors fled their homeland when undergoing religious and political persecution and established a new community in a land where they were granted religious and cultural freedom, only to flee again decades later when they were again being oppressed.

Another click in my brain occurred when I realized I had one more trait in common with all the attendees of the reunion. I had assumed that some of them were born and raised in Germany and their direct ancestors had been in Germany throughout the centuries. Not true. All of us in the reunion group descended from the Germans who had been born and worked in Bessarabia. The difference between me and

Wine, Bach, and Cuckoo Clocks

Gerhard, Peter, or Ulrich was that their ancestors returned to Germany after fleeing Russia. Mine came to North America.

That's what has brought us all together this weekend. We are all descendants of those people who were kicked out of one country and then another until finally settling where we all now live. My great-grandpa chose to come to Canada, but many of his cousins, second cousins, nieces, and nephews chose to go back to Germany instead. None of them had ever set foot in their chosen lands before migrating, yet they set out on faith that their new home would be better than the only one they had known previously. How brave our ancestors must have been, and how incredible that those of us in this room today all have that common background. I'm sure the ancestors are looking down in wonder, smiling at how we have found each other and that through modern travel and technology, we can remain connected, even though our family was torn apart so long ago by turmoil, war, migration, and hardship.

I looked around the room at the twenty or so faces and smiled.

Some of these people travelled two or three hours by car or train, others like Ulrich and his family live here in town or nearby, and the four of us from Canada travelled across an ocean to be here. We all gathered this weekend for the same reason: seeking out each other and our common past. Despite living in different countries, speaking different languages, these people are my family.

Afterword

I lived in Japan for three years in my early twenties and travelled to several other countries in Asia as well as Mexico, Jamaica, and Peru, but going to Germany was my first visit to a non-English-speaking country where I wasn't a visible minority. When I landed in Frankfurt the first time, I was accustomed to standing out from the locals with my medium-brown hair and large blue eyes, and I was conditioned to fumbling my way through a country while people forgave my linguistic blunders because they could see that I was clearly not a local. I was pleasantly surprised when some German tourists stopped me in the streets of Heilbronn to ask me, in German, for directions to the local tourist information office. My excitement got the better of me; I got my vocabulary mixed up and proudly gave them perfect directions to the train station.

My mom had travelled little and wasn't as knowledgeable about other cultures as I was, so she deferred to me for all decisions throughout our German adventure. I was confident getting us around, but being asked in a language I had only basic command of by people who thought I was local took me off guard and I had to stop and process what had happened.

"They think I'm German!" I realized, and I smiled widely. Unlike other countries I had travelled to, Germany welcomed me as if I were a local, and I subsequently felt as though I had found "my people." With this minor emotional breakthrough, I gained more confidence through that first trip and became bolder in trying out my weak German. People were forgiving and welcoming, and they seemed interested in talking to a Canadian who looked like them and was trying to speak their language. It still saddens me that I ran out of words when talking to an older man at the Heilbronn train station when Mom and I were headed back to Frankfurt at the end of our vacation, so we had to end the conversation long before our train arrived. Like my great-grandpa, he was a soft-spoken man I would have loved to chat with for much longer.

The warmth and familiarity I feel from people in Germany may be—as a result of my search for belonging—more of a construct I built in my mind than the reality, but that first trip was my homecoming. Even though Mom and I never found family names on any of the headstones, traipsing through that scenic town in central Germany with her and being received as a local connected me to a piece of myself I had been wanting to find since my earliest memories of sitting at my great-grandpa's feet, looking into those blue eyes of his, wondering what stories were locked behind them.

I still don't know how or even if I'm connected to the Stübers in Bacharach. I know I have relatives on both my parents' sides scattered throughout Germany, Austria, and elsewhere in the world, especially in the Canadian and American prairies. Most of my closest relatives are within a three-hour drive from where I live, and I don't know if those other two possible connections that were revealed to me at the family reunion are true familial ties. I've looked into this, but I don't have the right documents to confirm or dispute that I may be related to myself three different ways, nor do the family members here in Canada who I've asked.

But I found my family in those who attended the reunion.

And I also have, as a friend of mine says, a "chosen family" in Germany. Christine, Alan, Christine's parents, Markus, Annett, Sarah, and Julia have all embraced me for close to thirty years now (Sarah and Julia for as many of those thirty years as they've been alive), and every time I get off the plane in Frankfurt I know that I've arrived in my ancestral home.

Acknowledgements

I'm sure a lot of readers skip over the acknowledgements in books, but it's an important section because even though writing and publishing a book can be a lonely journey in large chunks along the way, having the right people in place for each book at the right time is imperative.

Firstly, thanks to my cover designer. I receive a lot of positive feedback on the covers of my books, and I'm also pleased with not only the product but also the process. The designers and support team at Miblart are fantastic to deal with. Thank you Tania, Nadia, and your team for your consistently excellent work and communication!

Janice helped with reminding me of details of certain adventures that I had forgotten, such as the fact that she went through an entire box of Kleenex at the Dr. Loosen winery. It's often said that we remember awful events if they happen to us but not if they happen to other people. I have clear memories of my experience with The Baltic Plague, but by the time her worst days came around, I was on the mend and merely grateful to be able to breathe for the rest of our trip.

Christine has, of course, been invaluable in the decades of our friendship for giving me great insight into what growing up in the former East Germany was like for her and how her family fared. I try not to pry, but when she opens the door, I ask what I feel I can without overstepping as I've always been interested in what life was like in these hidden countries during my formative years. Having grown up during the Cold War, my impressions were naturally the result of propaganda, and I'm still seeking to replace rumours with facts, including my impression that the countries that were behind the Wall were to be feared and distrusted.

Christine has also done a splendid job as tour guide on my many trips to Germany, taking me to places I would have never otherwise thought of going, such as the Herr Käthe Restaurant in Torgau. I will always be a hick, but she keeps trying to get me cultured.

Several relatives have contributed to my knowledge of our family history: Marvin, Rick, Charmaine, Auntie Doreen, Marietta, Anke,

Heidrun, Peter, and Ernst have all answered questions and filled in some gaps for me. Many others have compiled and preserved documents showing information going back almost two thousand years in some cases. Thank you to all of those in my family, especially my mom and grandma, who have kept these records for me and future generations.

I always look forward to receiving my editors' feedback, mainly because it's necessary but also because I know there will be a few giggles in the mix. Kimmy Beach, thank you again for reminding me that I use certain words eighty-two times in my manuscript and "the ideal number is zero." Thank you for kicking me in the butt when it came to letting go of large chunks of content that definitely needed to get the boot. And thank you also for your honesty in reminding me that "beautiful" is subjective and what one person finds beautiful another may not. Here are two of your most appreciated comments on this manuscript:

1. "My clearest memory of walking through the Schwartzwald [Black Forest] in the 1980s is the stunning amount of dog shit I had to step over. Not so beautiful."

2. And regarding Neuschwanstein, "I've been in that castle, and I found it utterly gaudy and useless. It's undoubtedly ornate, but bleh."

Tracey Anderson, thank you for tightening up my sentences and prying some of my favourite words and punctuation out of this manuscript. I enjoyed and appreciated your personal comments. One of my favourites was "This sentence has such a Lorna vibe." Working with you is always fun and informative.

Rebecca H. Lee, my audiobook narrator, thank you for putting your voice to my words and bringing my stories alive for those who prefer to listen rather than read. I look forward to many future collaborations!

And to those of you who have read or listened to this and perhaps one or more of my other books, I'm deeply and sincerely grateful for your support.

About the Author

Lorna Stuber has a bachelor of education degree with a double major in English language arts and social studies education (University of Lethbridge), a diploma in education specializing in English as a second language curriculum and instruction (University of Calgary), and an editing certificate (Simon Fraser University). She spent her twenties teaching ESL in Fujisawa, Japan, and Calgary, Canada, and her thirties and forties teaching online high school English, social studies, foods and nutrition, and Aboriginal studies courses for the Calgary Board of Education. After resigning from her teaching position, she began full-time editing, writing, and ghostwriting. In 2023, Lorna was one of three editors selected as a finalist for the Tom Fairley Award for Editorial Excellence, presented by Editors Canada.

Lorna spends most of her money on plane tickets and accommodation in cool and often obscure travel destinations. When she is not helping others fine-tune their writing, she is snowshoeing, volunteering for a local theatre, working on her own writing, and fulfilling her duties as a self-appointed "bad-influence auntie" to her friends' kids. She is the owner of Lorna Stuber—Editor, Proofreader, Writer.

Lorna currently lives in Okotoks, Canada, with her dust elephants and her kitchen view of the Rocky Mountains.

Website: lornastuber.com

Facebook: facebook.com/lornastubereditor

LinkedIn: linkedin.com/in/lorna-stuber-freelance-editor-writer-ghostwriter

Instagram: instagram.com/stuberlm/

Also by Lorna Stuber

Non-Fiction, Business
    The Fresh Freelancer
    Debt-Free at Forty-Three

Memoir
    Living My Golden Dream
    Nut Bags and Num-Nums

Voyages under the Midnight Sun

The following is a blog entry on my website. I'm including it here as a sneak preview to my next book, which will be about my travels in Greenland and Iceland. In the next book, which doesn't yet have a working title, I've pulled apart this blog and scattered the information in it throughout different chapters, expanding on the events in the blog.

You can sign up for my newsletter and blog here: https://lornastuber.com/m/create-account

Our big, beautiful planet is home to so many wonders, both man-made and natural. As a youngster, I made it a priority to see as many of them as possible on my short time on Earth. Greenland's drift ice and icebergs reminded me that nature is so much bigger and longer lasting than one human lifetime.

Three days into my two-week travels in Greenland in July 2024, we were told that we may not be able to get to the next town on our itinerary (Qaqortoq) because the drift ice was so thick. Greenland has no roads between towns and villages; modern options for getting from place to place are by boat or, if there are airports, by plane. After a couple hours in the lounge at our hostel, we were told that the boat captain was good to go and we needed to go *now*.

As we made the two-hour boat ride, I clenched my teeth and fists, wondering if our motorized and covered eleven-passenger boat was going to get stuck in the middle of the countless chunks of ice in the fjord. Our tour guide admitted she had never experienced travelling through such a heavy ice floe as we were going through on that nail-biting boat trip.

The journey felt like we were going through a maze, with the captain choosing one route and finding out that we were blocked. He then had to maneuver through a different path or—and I didn't even know this was possible—in some cases, go *over* the ice. I kept telling myself not to think about the Titanic, but the more I tried not to think about the Titanic, the more I did ... and how I have always thought that for me, the worst way to die would be by drowning.

We made it safely to Qaqortoq and back out of its harbour three days later after touring the town and hiking to the top of a small hill to view the icy fjord. Our journey continued up the western coast.

Two-hundred-fifty kilometres north of the Arctic Circle, off the coast of Ilulissat, is one of the world's many spectacular natural wonders: the Ilulissat Ice Fjord. This UNESCO World Heritage Site features gargantuan icebergs that dance and twinkle under the midnight sun before moving west to Newfoundland.

Whether you're in a boat putt-puttering among these showstoppers or viewing them from the air or shore, it's easy to see why this part of the world deserves to be preserved. Some of the icebergs are as long as two football fields; others can reach up to 300 feet above the sea (keep in mind that 90 percent of an iceberg is underwater).

I took an evening iceberg cruise to view these wonders up close. I also splurged on a helicopter ride, where I joined nine other travellers, flying from the Ilullisat airport to get aerial views of these massive icebergs and to see the glacier that calves[27] them.

Our pilot landed a couple hundred metres from the Sermeq Kujalleq glacier, one of the world's most active glaciers. According to UNESCO, every year, it calves more than "35 km^3 of ice, i.e. 10 percent of the production of all Greenland calf ice and more than any other glacier outside Antarctica."[28]

We stopped for half an hour to meander closer to the glacier, take photos, and enjoy some sparkling wine.

While I didn't walk on the Sermeq glacier, two days later I was hiking (with a sprained ankle!) on a different glacier, where Greenland's ice sheet meets the Tasiusaq Fjord system.

To get to this glacier, we left the small village of Ilimanaq (a forty-five minute boat ride south from Illulisat) by speedboat and crossed the first section of the fjord. My travel companions and I then bounced around in the back of an ATV on a hilly and rocky trail to the next part of the fjord and took another speedboat to a sandy beach at the foot of the glacier. Donning crampons, we crunched and climbed for thirty minutes to reach a higher vantage point where we could scan the seemingly never-ending ice sheet that stretches out in all directions. The thirty-minute trek back seemed more difficult than the hike up, probably because my ankle was starting to complain.

We spent one night in the cozy cabins of the Ilimanaq Lodge, which overlooks the ocean. From my cabin's front window, I could see two large icebergs directly in front of me. While I was resting up before dinner, staring at the glorious view, one of the icebergs started to move. I knew that icebergs are like living things, constantly melting, cracking, splitting, shifting, and drifting, but this one was on a mission! It scooted as if it were a boat that had just left the dock. I looked far into the distance, west, in the direction of Newfoundland, where I knew some of these icebergs would end up one, two, or three years from now. As I looked back and forth between the icebergs that were already miles into their journey, I imagined this closer one personified, as if it were looking out at its buddies far ahead, calling out in Icebergese, "Hey, wait up! I'm coming!" as it scurried toward them.

The spectacular Arctic scenery in Greenland prompted me to ponder the constant evolving of our beautiful planet—the changes we can and can't see in real time. I've visited numerous infamous archaeological sites worldwide, but as we all know, the Sphinx doesn't look the same today as it did when it was built. It's not a living creature, but erosion, weather, time, and human influence have caused changes in its features, as well as in countless other World Heritage sites.

Likewise, these icebergs are not stagnant. They may look the same over two or three days, but over years, months, or even weeks, the view in the Illulisat Ice Fjord and other coastal regions will change.

I've not been to Newfoundland, but I know that the icebergs there, and the one that the Titanic hit, were born in Greenland. The circle of life applies to these alive-but-not pieces of nature as well. Perhaps I should plan a visit to Newfoundland in a couple of years to welcome to Canada the beauties I saw in Greenland.

Endnotes

[1] "The Manifesto," The Volga Germans, accessed August 18, 2024, https://www.volgagermans.org/history/manifesto.

[2] "16 June 1871—Tsar Alexander II Revokes German Colonists' Privileges," Germans from Russia Settlement Locations, accessed February 25, 2025, https://www.germansfromrussiasettlementlocations.org/2019/06/16-june-1871-tsar-alexander-ii-revokes.html.

[3] "Germans From Russia Emigration and Immigration," Family Search, last modified August 12, 2024, 13:49, https://www.familysearch.org/en/wiki/Germans_from_Russia_Emigration_and_Immigration.

[4] "Wikipedia: August II the Strong," Wikimedia Foundation, last modified Sept 17, 2022, 01:57 (UTC), https://en.wikipedia.org/wiki/Augustus_II_the_Strong.

[5] "Wikipedia: Auerbachs Keller," Wikimedia Foundation, accessed August 20, 2024, 15:06 (UTC), https://en.wikipedia.org/wiki/Auerbachs_Keller.

[6] "The Unforgettable Story of the Nuremberg Sausage," Inside the TravelLab, accessed February 25, 2025, https://www.insidethetravellab.com/nuremberg-sausage/.

[7] "Neuschwanstein Castle Is A Disney Inspiration Desiged By A Mad King," Discovery, accessed February 25, 2025, https://www.discovery.com/exploration/neuschwanstein-castle-is-a-disney-inspiration-designed-by-a-mad-.

[8] "Wikipedia: Kraków Ghetto," Wikimedia Foundation, last modified August 26, 2022, 00:43 (UTC), https://en.wikipedia.org/wiki/Krak%C3%B3w_Ghetto.

[9] M. Jafiszow, Pawel Kubisztal, Grzegorz Szydlo eds., *Ghetto Heroes Square*, Krakow, 2010, p23-24.

[10] Jafiszow, Kubisztal, and Grzegorz p25-27.

[11] "The Eagle Pharmacy," KRAKOW.WIKI, accessed February 25, 2025, https://krakow.wiki/the-eagle-pharmacy/.

[12] "Top 20 St. Petersburg attractions and experiences," SAINT-PETERSBURG.COM, accessed February 25, 2025, http://www.saint-petersburg.com/top-20-attractions/.

[13] "Top 20 St. Petersburg attractions and experiences."

[14] "Top 20 St. Petersburg attractions and experiences."

[15] "Top 20 St. Petersburg attractions and experiences."

[16] "Definition of baltic," The Online Slang Dictionary, last edited October 1, 2001, http://onlineslangdictionary.com/meaning-definition-of/baltic.

[17] Propeller Island, accessed February 25, 2025, http://www.propeller-island.de/english/2/5/.

[18] Propeller Island City Lodge, accessed October 5, 2023, http://www.propeller-island.de/rooms_neu/room_detail/12/index.php.

[19] "Maps, analysis and statistics about the resident population, AdminStat Germania, accessed October 5, 2023, https://ugeo.urbistat.com/AdminStat/en/de/demografia/dati-sintesi/leiwen/20169148/4.

[20] "A Brief History of Glühwein, Germany's Favourite Christmas Drink," culture trip, accessed February 25, 2025, https://theculturetrip.com/europe/germany/articles/a-brief-history-of-gluhwein-germanys-favorite-christmas-drink/.

[21] "Oct 31, 1756: Giacomo Casanova Breaks out of Prison," ODD SALON, accessed February 25, 2025, https://oddsalon.com/jan-5-1757-giacomo-casanova-breaks-out-of-prison/.

[22] "Wikipedia: St. Peter's Basilica," Wikimedia Foundation, last modified October 13, 2022, 05:59 (UTC), https://en.wikipedia.org/wiki/St._Peter%27s_Basilica.

[23] "Melanchthon House," Luther Museen, accessed October 5, 2024, https://www.luthermuseen.de/en/museen/melanchthon-house.

[24] J. P. Romney and Rebecca Romney, *Printer's Error: Irreverent Stories from Book History*, Harper Collins, New York 2017 First Edition, p54-55.

[25] "Wikipedia: Schupfnudel," Wikimedia Foundation, last modified April 23, 2023, 16:56 (UTC), https://en.wikipedia.org/wiki/Schupfnudel.

[26] "Wikipedia: Swabians," Wikimedia Foundation, last modified January 3, 2025, 21:13 (UTC), https://en.wikipedia.org/wiki/Swabians.

[27] *Calving* is when large chucks of ice break off of the end of a glacier, creating icebergs. Active glaciers calve; dead glaciers no longer produce icebergs.

[28] "Illulissat Icefjord," UNESCO, accessed August 22, 2024, https://whc.unesco.org/en/list/1149/.

www.ingramcontent.com/pod-product-compliance
Lightning Source LLC
Chambersburg PA
CBHW020532080526
44583CB00013B/835